TWAYNE'S WORLD AUTHORS SERIES

A Survey of the World's Literature

Sylvia E. Bowman, Indiana University

GENERAL EDITOR

SPAIN

Gerald E. Wade, Vanderbilt University

EDITOR

Benjamín Jarnés

(TWAS 128)

TWAYNE'S WORLD AUTHORS SERIES (TWAS)

The purpose of TWAS is to survey the major writers—novelists, dramatists, historians, poets, philosophers, and critics—of the nations of the world. Among the national literatures covered are those of Australia, Canada, China, Eastern Europe, France, Germany, Greece, India, Italy, Japan, Latin America, New Zealand, Poland, Russia, Scandinavia, Spain, and the African nations, as well as Hebrew, Yiddish, and Latin Classical literatures. This survey is complemented by Twayne's United States Authors Series and English Authors Series.

The intent of each volume in these series is to present a critical-analytical study of the works of the writer; to include biographical and historical material that may be necessary for understanding, appreciation, and critical appraisal of the writer; and to present all material in clear, concise English—but not to vitiate the scholarly content of the work by doing so.

THIS IS POOR

Benjamín Jarnés

By J. S. BERNSTEIN

The City College of The City
University of New York

Twayne Publishers, Inc. :: New York

For
Maxine
and
Jeffrey Alexander

Preface

Benjamín Jarnés published his first book in 1924, and soon joined the editorial board of the *Revista de Occidente.* For the next twelve years, his prolific production of novels, essays and biographies seemed to exemplify certain of the artistic ideals enunciated by Ortega y Gasset in his much discussed *La deshumaniza-ción del arte (The Dehumanization of Art).* At the end of the Spanish Civil War, Jarnés moved to Mexico where he continued writing. In 1948 he returned to Spain. Before his death in August, 1949, two more of his books were published in Barcelona.

This study reviews Jarnés' major essays and works of fiction with a view to clarifying some of the issues raised by the aesthetics of dehumanization. Attention is paid to the debate on the novel and to the defects Jarnés was charged with by his critics. Although they are inherently interesting, I have not dealt with the biographies because of the limitations of space. In my examinations of the novels, I have placed relatively more emphasis on thematic, structural and symbolic matters than on verbal style.

In my discussion of Jarnés' writings, I have often made reference to important works by other authors in Spain and elsewhere. Where pertinent I have tried to specify similarities between Jarnés and other writers with some detail.

No adequate biography of our author has as yet been published. Until a competent biographer appears, I have had to hold in abeyance certain inquiries I would like to have made into such things as the proper weight which should be accorded to Jarnés' biography in the estimation of his work, and the influence on him of personal acquaintances, of travel in Spain and abroad, and of specific events in Spanish and world history.

In a short study of such a large corpus, certain aspects must unfortunately be slighted. I hope that this book may serve as an inducement to others to bring some of the areas of Jarnés' output which I have neglected into sharper focus. I also hope that those who follow me will correct my mistakes and shed light on the aspects which I found only obscure.

J. S. BERNSTEIN

Mexico City
Spring, 1969

Contents

Chronology

1888   October 7: Benjamín Jarnés Millán born in Codo (Zaragoza).

1898   Schooling at the Pontifical University and the San Carlos Seminary.

1908   Leaves the seminary.

1910   Enters the Army Administrative Corps Reserve; concurrently prepares for a teaching career at the Zaragoza Normal School.

1916   Marries Gregoria Bergua.

1919   Stationed in Larache, Morocco.

1920   Returns to Madrid where he settles permanently.

1923   Contributes to *Alfar* [La Coruña]; in September, the coup d'état of Primo de Rivera; *Revista de Occidente* begins publication.

1924   *Mosén Pedro (Father Pedro)*; Unamuno exiled by Primo de Rivera.

1925   Publishes for the first time in the *Revista de Occidente*, a story entitled "El río fiel" ("The Faithful River"); also publishes Paul Tuffrau's *Leyenda de Guillermo de Orange (The Legend of William of Orange)*, translated from French.

1926   *El profesor inútil (The Useless Professor)*, his first novel; writes regularly for *La Vanguardia* [Barcelona] and *La Gaceta Literaria* [Madrid]; Unamuno's *Cómo se hace una novela*; Valle-Inclán's *Tirano Banderas*.

1927   *Ejercicios (Exercises)*; the war in Morocco ends; Góngora tercentenary.

1928   *El convidado de papel (The Paper Guest)*; *Leyendas polacas (Polish Legends)*, translation of Polish tales by Susana Strowska; Lorca's *Romancero gitano*; Jorge Guillén's *Cántico*.

1929   *Locura y muerte de nadie (The Madness and Death of
        Nobody); Paula y Paulita (Paula and Paulette); Salón de
        estío (Summer Salon); Sor Patrocinio (Sister Patrocinius);*
        translates Remarque's *Im Westen nicht Neues (All Quiet
        on the Western Front);* joins the editorial board of *La
        Gaceta Literaria;* with Guillermo de Torre edits *La Gaceta
        Americana;* Primo de Rivera closes the universities; Lorca
        in New York.

1930   *Teoría del zumbel (Theory of the Top-String); Viviana y
        Merlín: leyenda (The Legend of Vivien and Merlin);* dicta-
        torship of Primo de Rivera ends; Ortega y Gasset's *La
        rebelión de las masas.*

1931   *Escenas junto a la muerte (Scenes on the Brink of Death);
        Rúbricas: nuevos ejercicios (Flourishes: New Exercises);
        Zumalacárregui: el caudillo romántico (Zumalacárregui:
        The Romantic Chieftain);* Alfonso XIII leaves Spain for
        Italy; Second Republic proclaimed on April 14; Ortega,
        Pérez de Ayala, and Marañón form the League of Intel-
        lectuals in Defense of the Republic.

1932   *Lo rojo y lo azul: homenaje a Stendhal (The Red and the
        Blue: Homage to Stendhal); Sobre la gracia artística (On
        Artistic Grace);* translates Philippe's *Bubu de Montpar-
        nasse (Bubu of Montparnasse);* Anarchist disturbances;
        Bergamín founds *Cruz y Raya.*

1933   *Fauna contemporánea (Contemporary Animal Life);* Fal-
        angist party founded by Primo de Rivera's son, José
        Antonio; Lorca's *Bodas de sangre.*

1934   *Cardenio: monodrama (Cardenius: Monodrama); Vida de
        San Alejo (The Life of St. Alexis);* increasing political
        strife in Asturias and Catalonia; Lorca's *Yerma.*

1935   *Castelar: hombre del Sinaí (Castelar: The Man from the
        Sinai); Feria del libro (Book Fair); Libro de Esther (The
        Book of Esther); Tántalo: farsa (Tantalus: A Farce);*
        Unamuno made "honorary citizen" of the Republic;
        Dámaso Alonso's *La lengua poética de Góngora.*

1936   *Cita de ensueños: figuras del cinema (A Date with Illu-
        sion: Movie Personalities); Doble agonía de Bécquer (The
        Double Agony of Becquer); Don Alvaro o la fuerza del
        tino (Don Alvaro or the Power of Good Aim);* Franco pro-
        nounces in Morocco and the Civil War begins on July 18;

Revista de Occidente and *Cruz y Raya* suspend publication; deaths of Lorca, Unamuno, and Valle-Inclán.

1939 Civil War ends in Franco's victory, April 1; Jarnés leaves Spain for exile in Mexico, arriving in June.

1940 *Cartas al Ebro: biografía y crítica (Letters to the Ebro: Biography and Criticism); La novia del viento (The Wind's Sweetheart);* Jarnés is literary editor of *Hoy* and *Mañana* in Mexico City.

1942 *Don Vasco de Quiroga: obispo de Utopía (Vasco de Quiroga: Bishop of Utopia); Escuela de libertad: siete maestros (School for Freedom: Seven Teachers); Manuel Acuña: poeta de su siglo (Manuel Acuña: Poet of His Age); Orlando el pacífico (Orlando the Calm); Stefan Zweig: cumbre apagada, retrato (Stefan Zweig: Portrait of a Departed Master);* Jarnés teaches at the Normal School and the National University in Mexico City; Cela's *La familia de Pascual Duarte.*

1943 *Venus dinámica (Dynamic Venus).*

1944 *Cervantes: bosquejo biográfico (Cervantes: A Biographical Sketch); Constelación de Friné (Friné's Constellation),* under the pseudonym of Julio Aznar; publishes two translations from French, Gourmont's *Historias mágicas (Magic Tales),* and Périot's *Temperamento y personalidad (Temperament and Personality);* Laforet's *Nada.*

1945 Publishes two more translations from French, Germain's *Los paraísos (Paradises),* and Prévost's *Historia de Manon Lescaut y del Caballero del Grieux (The Story of Manon Lescaut and the Knight of Grieux).*

1946 *Ariel disperso (Ariel in Flight);* the review *Insula* founded in Madrid.

1948 *Eufrosina o la gracia (Euphrosyne or Grace);* returns to Spain; Américo Castro's *España en su historia.*

1949 August 10: Dies in Madrid.

CHAPTER 1

Life and Times

I Childhood, Youth and Manhood

B ENJAMÍN Jarnés Millán was born in Codo, Zaragoza, on
October 7, 1888, the seventeenth of twenty-two children. His
father, Pedro Jarnés, was a tailor whose first wife gave him fourteen children. When she died he married Bernabea Millán, Benjamín's mother, who gave him eight more. We know very little
about the family; everything which has been written about it supports Jarnés' own description of their poverty. By his own account
his childhood was unhappy, for no one bothered about him. "I
was probably just another mouth to feed, an economic burden. . . .
Of course, I didn't consume a great deal of tenderness; no one
gave me any; especially at home, there was hardly any supply of
affection. Because poverty very quickly does away with it."[1]
Whether because of his unhappy childhood or because of a belief
in the artistic irrelevance of personal details, Jarnés seldom allowed autobiographical material to enter directly into his novels.
While we can glimpse the author behind a great many of his
fictional heroes, and while various episodes from the novels are
autobiographical in origin, Jarnés was loath to deal with the
obviously autobiographical or the deeply personal interior lives
of his characters.

On one occasion when he did so, however, he defended his
right to recast the details of his past life on the grounds that,
since the artist is free to choose his subject matter, he is also free
to find autobiography uncongenial or unsuitable, and to disdain
it.[2] As we shall see, the details of his own life, just as Jarnés'
experiences of others and of the world around him, were all subjected to a process of artistic censorship before they were granted
admission into his work. This should not seem unusual, since he
remembered his home life as deprived economically and emotionally.

Some of his earliest remembered experiences involved books. Many of the books in his father's library were tattered volumes which lacked several pages at the beginning or the end. Jarnés' ambition was to invent beginnings and endings for these volumes, supply through imagination what reality lacked (*ibid.*, p. 15). It would not be too much to state that this activity was to become a hallmark of his literary approach, for as we shall see, reality in itself was always an insufficient basis for his fiction. Rather, it was reality transformed, added to, manipulated, intellectualized, which was the material for his writing. Further, the shapes of his novels are such as to permit the addition of new fictional material at their beginnings or ends; his fictions are all open-ended.

An early ambition concerning books was to possess a library of finely-bound, expensive-looking editions like those the priest had. His father had apparently been a man of literary pretensions. But the better books of his library had had to be sold to pay debts.

In addition to his interest in the tools of scholarship, Jarnés quite early displayed a certain inclination for learning. In the family album, his godmother had written of him: "This boy, at five and a half, knew how to read in all the books, and he was taught catechism lessons, and he learned them by heart overnight" (*ibid.*, p. 17). It is likely that his response to the catechism lessons stemmed from his receiving daily attention from his elders rather than from innate piety.

Jarnés wrote that his earliest memory, which he dates sometime before 1895, is of his father receiving a visit from a man who wanted to sell some books. "My father received him coldly, but the traveller, very politely, opened his package and showed him a large lot of brand-new books, beautiful little red, green, yellow books; thicker books bound in black leather, with gold lettering, like the priest's" (*ibid.*, p. 16). The salesman said how very cheap the books were, but the father became enraged. The young Benjamín stood by, coveting the books, wanting to handle and caress them. "But suddenly, rudely, my father rejected the books; he hurled a sentence at the traveller's face . . . I remember it, I remember it perfectly; but I don't want to say it: one still cannot say these things in Spain. For the first time I heard the name of Luther. The poor traveller wrapped up his wares and left. I also remember what he said in farewell, but I must not repeat that either: one still cannot say these things in Spain. He left, taking with him my eyes, my hands, my childish eagerness to caress for once a pretty toy: a book, a brand-new book, with shiny gold letters."

This memory is quite revealing. First of all, it provides additional corroboration, if any were needed, of the persistence in many rural areas of Spain at the end of the century of the sort of hermetic Catholicism described by George Borrow in *The Bible in Spain* (1843). The roots of the attitude of Jarnés' father, its phobic quality, have been the subject of considerable discussion, and are in fact to be seen still in Spain.[3] In the second place, the memory illustrates Jarnés' precocious sympathy for the man considered a heretic or deviate. The sympathy is not based on any high-principled love of freedom; a boy under seven years of age could hardly have felt any. Rather it is founded on a clear reaction of the younger Jarnés against his father's discourtesy and authoritarian manner, and on the fact that his father was sending away the man who possessed what Jarnés most highly valued. Thirdly, we remark that as the salesman carried away his books, he took with him Jarnés' desire for the books, not as vehicles for marvelous undiscovered worlds, but as toys or objects to be possessed.

The book as toy or game is a theme which will occupy us later in this study, for it was to become one of the constant themes of Jarnés' aesthetics. It embodies an irreverence toward the printed text, an agnoticism, so to speak, which is transformed, in the author's artistic credo, into a certain intellectual distance from the literary work. The theme also stresses the notion of gaiety or joy which Jarnés came to consider one of the mainsprings of his own fiction.

Let us also notice that the memory of the bookseller involves little direct action on the part of the young Jarnés. He is an observer of the event, but does not protest to his father the latter's treatment of the salesman. Nor does he do any more than express a certain sympathy for the man ill used by his father. Here also we find a trait which will come to characterize Jarnés' fictional production and a number of his fictional heroes as well: the condition of spectator rather than of participant. In fact, Jarnés tells us of this when he says: "I remember each period of my childhood by the height of the things I used to sit on; some might remember theirs by the height of the things they liked to climb on."[4] In quite clear fashion, Jarnés has drawn the distinction between the aggressive, upwardly-striving participant in, and the sedentary spectator of, the world around him. And while his literary career was not to be entirely that of either the one or the other, the spectator usually predominated.

He summed up his childhood some years later in a passage in one of his notebooks: "I was still a child when I left what might have been my home, but I already carried with me the painful scar of neglect, contempt, perhaps of hatred, which I will never be able to erase, even using all the procedures of forgetfulness and kindness."[5] He left home for the Pontifical University in Zaragoza. There, and at the San Carlos Seminary, he acquired the fundamentals of humanistic education, of philosophy and of theology.[6] He learned and retained his Latin so well that fifteen years later, he was able to give private lessons in the subject. His experiences in the Seminary provide some of the material for his second novel, *El convidado de papel* (*The Paper Guest*), 1928. They also helped confirm the lack of vocation which was to keep him from being ordained.[7]

He attended the Pontifical University and the Seminary until 1908. Two years later he entered the Army; he served in the Administrative Corps Reserve and for a number of years considered making the Army his career.[8] Concurrently, he studied for a teaching career at the Zaragoza Normal School; though he graduated he never held any teaching appointment until his exile in Mexico. We may safely assume that his moving toward teaching was motivated primarily by the need to supplement his Army pay.[9]

In 1916, while still in the Army, Jarnés married Gregoria Bergua, like himself from the region of Aragón. The following year he was posted to Zaragoza and, in 1918, to the city of Jaca in the neighboring province of Huesca. In 1919, he was sent to Larache in Morocco, whence he returned in the following year to settle permanently in Madrid.

II *Literary Maturity*

One of the most frustrating facts for the student of Jarnés is that published biographies of him tell us almost nothing about the years of his youth and young manhood. We know nothing about his days at the university in Zaragoza, nor about the years he spent in the Army. It is possible to assume that some of the material in *Lo rojo y lo azul (The Red and the Blue)*, 1932, is autobiographical, for the setting is an army barracks. But in the decade between 1910 and 1920, that is, the period when Jarnés had come to maturity in both his personal and intellectual life, the lacunae in published information are almost total.[10]

In 1917, he began contributing articles to a Catholic magazine in Zaragoza, *El Pilar*. Occasionally, he wrote for *Rosas y Espinas*, a publication of the Dominican Order in Valencia. Very little is known of these articles, most likely Jarnés' earliest published work, because of the limited circulation and audience of the magazines in which they appeared.[11] By 1923, he was contributing to the "little magazine" *Alfar*, in La Coruña. The following year, his first published book appeared, *Mosén Pedro (Father Pedro)*, a portrait of a rural priest.[12]

In 1925, in conjunction with Valentín Andrés Alvarez, Guillermo de Torre, and others, Jarnés founded *Plural*. In this magazine he published "El río fiel" ("The Faithful River"), a section of his first novel, *El profesor inútil (The Useless Professor)*, which appeared the following year. This fragment from his novel, and a section of Alvarez' novel, *Sentimental Dancing*, were brought to the attention of Ortega y Gasset, founder and director of the *Revista de Occidente* which was already at that time Spain's most prestigious cultural and literary review. Ortega invited Jarnés and Alvarez to contribute to his review, and Jarnés shortly joined the staff as a paid contributor of fiction and book reviews.[13] He was to continue writing for the *Revista* until 1936 when, with the outbreak of the Civil War, it suspended publication.

The most active and innovative period of Jarnés' career began in 1925. His literary friendships with Ortega, Guillermo de Torre, and others accompanied an abundant production, and he soon was considered part of the "New Literature." From 1926 on, Jarnés was a regular contributor to *La Vanguardia* of Barcelona, and to *La Gaceta Literaria* of Madrid. His book reviews and other journalistic writings make up an activity which was to continue unabated until 1936; their frequency would diminish only with the Civil War and Jarnés' subsequent exile in Mexico.

The majority of Jarnés' novels appeared before 1933, and it is on the basis of their contribution to the renovation of novelistic prose that Jarnés' reputation primarily rests. His work after that year came increasingly to be made up of biographies and short stories. Several of his novels were reissued in enlarged versions. Despite his wide renown and continued productivity, Jarnés seems never to have been entirely convinced that he had won a secure place for himself in literature. In a letter to Walter Pabst, the German Hispanist, he wrote: "I suffer periods of great depression in which I think myself an insignificant writer, or almost that."[14] In the opinion of many, however, Jarnés was far from insignificant. Ricardo Gullón, in a short article published after the author's death, related how helpful and generous he had always been to younger writers, how he was always willing to help launch or sustain a new magazine with a literary contribution.[15] Gullón reports that at the beginning of the 1930's, Jarnés was often to be found writing five or six different articles for various newspapers and reviews.

The self-doubt which was present in varying intensity throughout most of Jarnés' literary maturity may have been partially a result of his less-than-favored position in his own family. A writer who recalls his childhood as a period when he was largely ignored and unloved may reasonably think himself subject to similar neglect or unworthy of praise in adulthood. His family were persuaded of his importance as a writer only after seeing his copy of another author's book with the author's handwritten dedication to Jarnés.[16] What is of paramount importance here is not whether Jarnés' childhood was unhappy in fact, but rather that he chose to view it as such from the vantage point of maturity. Likewise, we are interested not in whether his family actually did not early acknowledge his literary accomplishments, but that our author says they did not. It should not surprise us, in addition, to see in Jarnés' literary career certain correspondences to his familial situation.

In the first place, Jarnés was no solitary figure in the literary landscape of his day. He was one—perhaps the leader—of a large number of writers who in the 1920's and 1930's brought to the novel a certain poetic tendency which sought to renovate prose. Literarily, he was no lone Romantic suffering an agony brought about by his isolation from, and the incomprehension of, his society. He issued no apocalyptic *pronunciamientos* on the death of the novel or of art. He participated with many others in the excitement the younger generation feels when it is certain it is surpassing its elders in literature. Rather than a monolithic and unique figure, he was firmly if not always comfortably a part of the group of admirers and disciples of Ortega y Gasset, some of whom were engaged in the creation of works similar to his.

Secondly, and more important, there is almost no contentiousness in Jarnés' views of either the literary scene or of other writers. If he had seen himself as a solitary, misunderstood pathfinder, discovering new directions for fiction, we would surely expect a polemical or disputatious tone, a few clear rivalries with other authors, perhaps one or two cordial enmities. But Jarnés' critical writings are largely filled with appreciations and compliments. Where he found his subject lacking or delinquent, a gentle reminder of the novelist's duties as he saw them, or a mild rebuke for insufficiencies, were usually enough.

Third, Jarnés' attitude toward his role in literature was marked by equanimity. He wrote: "There is no reason to lament anything or be thankful for anything; rather accept life just as it has been given to us, and accept it with its most pleasing outcomes. Fulfill our destiny gladly."[17] Surely the various careers Jarnés attempted before finding his place as a writer demanded patience and restraint in adversity. We never come upon a review or essay of his in which he can be seen ranting or delivering intemperate judgments. While criticisms of the Church, the Army, and the foibles of Spanish society abound in his works, they are almost always calm and considered, often humorous, and always lacking in the gripping sense of anguish which betrays an experience of personal suffering. Rather, even those passages most critical are tempered by his artistic censor.

One of the ways in which Jarnés managed challenging or dismaying experiences was to expose their inappropriate or humorous elements. Thus, commenting on the prevalence of the sort of writer whose grandiose claims to fame rest on one poem or short story, published and applauded only by his friends and family, together with a vast number of vague plans for further works which never come to be written, Jarnés wrote: "I have always been amused by watching the false writer; how he arises out of the void, how he develops, gesticulates, and dies" (*ibid.*, p. 24). In such writers, Jarnés criticizes the absence of seriousness, vocation and training, indirectly affirming his own sense of apprenticeship to the craft of writing, and his need to submit whatever he wrote to an internal censor. His self-censorship would often cause him to tear up what he had written. The "false writer," lacking a commitment to the vocation of writer, would not refine or polish. He was a *nouveau riche* in the world of letters.

Jarnés' sense of the seriousness of the vocation of writing was such that, after six years of publishing novels and articles, of occupying an important place in Spain's most important literary review, of being sought out for contributions to reviews in Spain and America, he still thought of himself as an apprentice.[18] The note of modesty in this opinion was to continue to exist throughout his career. Likewise, one of his fictional *personae,* recurring often in his works, and serving as the title of his best-known novel, was that of the *profesor inútil,* the useless teacher. This *persona* embodies both the notion of vocation and dedication in the role of writer, and of the pursuit of beauty for its own sake. The sense of dedication is related to Jarnés' experience in the seminary; his need for a vocation, at first misdirected toward a life as a priest, was satisfied as a writer. The vocation is still present, but now channelled into a secular occupation.

In the next chapter, we shall examine in some detail the importance of the idea of beauty for its own sake in our author's aesthetic. For the present, we should merely recall that attitudes opposed to mechanization and industrialization, to considering the utility of things their primary quality, were widespread in Spain and Europe in the 1920's and 1930's. The case for the maladapted man, presenting the brutality and anti-humane nature of a culture ruled by the demands of efficiency and utility, was made with full force by Charlie Chaplin. Jarnés, as did many others, took a certain pride in being unsuited to a mechanized society, constitutionally or otherwise unfit for devotion to the ideas of utility. The pride is also related to a pride in his craft as a writer, in the painstaking perfection of his skills, and to his stigmatizing "false writers." For these are all aspects of an aris-

tocratic leaning in Jarnés which was well developed in many
areas of his thinking on letters and life.

In 1929, Jarnés joined the editorial board of *La Gaceta Literaria*. In the same year, he and Guillermo de Torre assumed the
editorship of *La Gaceta Americana*. For this review, Jarnés
covered the Spanish literary and cultural scene, while Torre
reported on American affairs from Buenos Aires. In a report
of another literary banquet held that year, one honoring García
Lorca before his departure for New York, Torres Bodet has
given us a glimpse of Jarnés. He was "passionate and self-willed;
he suffered and enjoyed everything excessively. One could notice
in Benjamín Jarnés' intelligence a crease of snowy white—of
a surplice or altar cloth—which the seminary's irons impress on
the most singular talents."[19]

In September, 1930, Jarnés began writing a series of notebooks; they contained jottings and notes for future work, many
personal confessions, as well as aphorisms and quotations. Of
the thirty-eight notebooks he wrote up to the winter of 1943-44,
only twenty-nine have been preserved.[20] The notebooks apparently received a large part of the author's thinking about the convulsive social and political changes which, with the abdication
of Alfonso XIII and the proclamation of the Second Republic
in 1931, were occurring with dizzying speed. From what Fuentes
passes on of this material, we can see Jarnés' anguish at the
approaching political impasse. Where his published works in
this period betray almost no important concern in our author
with the events of an unusual nature which were occurring in
Spain, the notebooks convey strong democratic and anti-extremist
leanings. The democracy Jarnés invokes was to have a "mental
basis, that is, one of mutual comprehension and the acceptance
of human values."[21]

Despite what may seem now as naiveté and grandeur in this
notion, the position was a popular one in the early thirties. The
polemics centering on the Civil War tend to obscure the fact
that there were many who were political moderates, who were
no partisans of the use of force in the achievement of political
and social ends.

In the years of the Republic, in addition to writing novels,
essays and reviews, Jarnés was also among the founders of two
groups which enjoyed some importance before the Civil War.

One was the Group of Independent Film Writers, whose mission it was to review films, put together a library of important movies, and write on cinematic history. The Group set about a "labor of public orientation, sponsoring distinguished films."[22] As was true of many groups of official and private character during these years—e.g., Lorca's travelling theater group, La Barraca, to cite just one—the Group was carrying out one of the primary aims of the Republic's policy of public education; not only was the policy concerned with education in the formal sense, but also with increasing the awareness and involvement of the average man in his country's literature and culture.

The second group, perhaps less aimed at the general public than the first, but sharing a similar spirit, was the PEN Club, a literary association which carried on publishing activities. The first book issued under its auspices was Jarnés' *Vida de San Alejo* (*The Life of St. Alexis*) in 1934. Other authors either published or announced for publication at that time were Ricardo Gullón, Eugenio d'Ors, Fernando Vela, Valentín Andrés Alvarez and Torres Bodet.

Years of intense literary activity and productivity, the early 1930's augured well for Jarnés. Despite the pain of his rheumatism, and his periodic depressions, his output continued. He was one of a large number of writers who made a new literary Golden Age for Spain. There was reason to hope that the substantial cultural resurgence would continue in full force, gaining ever wider influence among the reading public, and reasserting in literature—as in the national life generally—the proof of Spain's viability and equality in the European community of nations.[23] The Civil War and its aftermath shattered that hope as it did so many others.

In the space of less than three years, the career which had taken ten to shape and nurture in Spain was broken off. Jarnés, as did many hundreds of other writers and intellectuals, found his activities disrupted by the war. The national crisis precluded *belles lettres*. In 1936, Jarnés who had been a Republican since the beginning of the Republic, assumed active service in the Army once more, now as an administrative officer in the Medical Corps.[24] Between 1936 and 1939, he also wrote regularly for *La Vanguardia* of Barcelona, and for *La Nación* of Buenos Aires, as chief of its "Spanish Literature" section. Two books,

both unpublished, deal with and were written during the war:
La casa de los pájaros (The Birds' House), a novel which was
still unfinished in 1942, and *Escombros (Ruins)*, travel sketches.[25]
Fuentes reports that the war's effect was to make Jarnés more
withdrawn, horrified by the cruelty and devastation which were
sweeping across Spain; presumably his notebooks shed light on
the details of this withdrawal. We know that the effect of the
early weeks of the war on Jarnés was to make him feel "dehumanized," for he was quoted by Ontañón as having said that
immediately after the war began "all my external movements
were so mechanical, indifferent, that . . . going and coming, eating and not eating, greeting [people] or not in this way or that,
in sum, everything took place in me without passing through
me. My arms, my legs, my lips, my eyes, my ears, even my very
stomach, were obeying a rhythm completely foreign to my own
rhythm . . . What was left of myself? At the time, I didn't even
ask myself. Some weeks went by without my being able to get
out of my painful stupor. That was the war!"[26]
The shock of the war, the urgent need Jarnés felt to serve the
Republican army in a useful way, reinforced his sympathies
for the Republican cause. When this cause was finally lost, he,
along with legions of compatriots, left Spain for exile.[27]

III *Exile and Return*

At the end of the Civil War in 1939, Jarnés and his wife fled
from Barcelona to France. After short visits in Limoges and
Paris, they went to Mexico.[28] The hardships implied by such a
flight, the severence of his professional associations, the con-
current loss of income and of facilities for earning a living,
were mitigated somewhat for Jarnés by the hospitality of some
Mexican friends. The difficulties of adjustment were nonetheless
severe.
He found employment as the literary editor of *Hoy*, and then of
its successor, *Mañana*. In 1940 and 1941, he was a frequent contributor of fiction, essays, and reviews to the magazines *Ro-
mance* and *España Peregrina*, which had been founded in Mexico
by Spanish emigrés.[29] Jarnés was no newcomer to Mexican literary reviews; he had published from time to time in the late
1920's in *Sagitario, Contemporáneos* and *Ulises*.
In exile, Jarnés continued publishing prolifically, biographies

and translations outnumbering fiction in his output. In addition
to three small anthologies of humor, Jarnés also edited a series
of children's books, and a six-volume encyclopedia of literature.
He taught Spanish Literature for a time at the Higher Normal
School in the capital, and was in charge of a summer course at
the National University which dealt with picaresque literature.

The economic hardship which he suffered undoubtedly played
a part in his undertaking several of the editorships mentioned
above, and in the increasing number of biographies in his output.
As we shall see in more detail in the next chapter, the events of
the Civil War and its European aftermath had made Jarnés'
works seem irrelevant because of his conscious avoidance of the
personal anecdote in his fiction, and his antipathy to the social
novel or, as it was called in Spain by hostile commentators, "the
novel of the masses." Jarnés' failing was not so much in the verbal
style of his novels—although many critics were to attack it—as
in the fact that he was unable or unwilling to draw upon the
events of his life in Spain during the Republic, the Civil War,
and his exile for material for his fiction.

But there is another element which may have caused the turn
to biography as a primary outlet for his talents. The fact of exile
from Spain implied for Jarnés as for his emigré compatriots a
severe break with his personal and national past. Deprived of
contact with his native country, uprooted abruptly at the height
of his career, he was impelled to examine the implications of his
exile, to analyze its causes. Like the analytical stance of the
writers of the Generation of 1898, one of whose most widespread
goals was to explain the roots of Spain's decline in the nineteenth
century, Jarnés' involved a looking backward, personally and
historically. In writing the life stories of Bolívar, Lincoln, San
Martín, Washington, Stefan Zweig, Manuel Acuña, Cervantes,
among others, Jarnés is symbolically writing his own life story.
He is turning his scrutiny to the historical trajectories of notable
individuals, perhaps because he could not turn it, due to the
principles of his aesthetics, upon his own. The biographer's impulse here, as elsewhere, implies a looking backward and in-
vestigation of "how it came about." This could be considered
an evasion, a deflection of Jarnés' attention from the fundamental
problem which concerned him: how it could come about that he
(and Spain) had suffered the radical crisis of the Civil War.[30]

This attitude is fairly common among the emigré writers. In the trilogies of Ramón Sender, *Crónica del alba*, and of Barea, *La forja de un rebelde*, in the novels of Max Aub and Manuel Lamana, in the stories of Francisco Ayala, there is a similar impetus to begin at the beginning. In Sender and Barea their beginning is in their childhood; for Ayala (e.g., in the story "El hechizado"), the beginning is in the history of Spain in the seventeenth century. In these novelists as well, there is the desire and ability to make novels out of their experiences during the Republic, the War, and their exile. The majority of the subjects of Jarnés' biographies lived in the nineteenth century or later. However, when he did turn to earlier figures, e.g., in his study of Vasco de Quiroga, we can perhaps see an interest in history and a symbolic search for the present pertinence of historical personalities.

The experience of exile was to be a fruitful one for many of the emigrés, helping to cure them of localism, and to bring them to a knowledge and love of America.[31] In the case of Jarnés these benefits were perhaps less marked than in others, for he had never been locally oriented in his intellectual outlook. He had for many years been a commentator on and reviewer of the works of Americans and Europeans. His exile did bring him direct knowledge of the American continent, but the effects of that knowledge are hardly discernible in his work. Where some of the exiles, chief among them Sender and Max Aub, incorporated Mexican and American scenes and themes into their fiction, Jarnés did not. The demands of his aesthetic canon were such as to exclude the possibility that the details of his personal experience might influence his writings.

Toward the middle of the 1940's, Jarnés, who had long suffered from a painful and at times debilitating rheumatism, developed arteriosclerosis which gradually paralyzed him completely.[32] In 1948 he returned to Spain. It was impossible for Jarnés to begin again, at sixty, to make a career. The works he had published in exile had gone largely unnoticed in Spain, a fate common to most of the literary works of the exiles.[33] His illness, the shock of discovering a Spain very different from the one he had left nine years before, must have made the last months of his life profoundly depressing. Two books appeared that year, *Eufrosina o la gracia (Euphrosyne or Grace)*, a reworking of some of the ideas set forth sixteen years earlier in *Sobre la gracia artística (On Artistic Grace)*, and a second edition of *Libro de Esther (The Book of Esther)*, essays on art.

Benjamín Jarnés died on August 10, 1949, in Madrid. His passing was unmarked by the Spanish literary world, except for a few brief obituaries.[34]

CHAPTER 2

The Dehumanization of Art

I *Jarnés' Novelistic Aesthetic*

"Literature is an art, the most considerable art, the supreme art."

—BENJAMIN JARNÉS[1]

THE fifteen years which preceded the Civil War were a period of intense literary activity in Spain. As in America and elsewhere in Europe, it was a time when a new generation of writers declared its existence, disavowing old ideals and standards, and proclaimed its coming of age by fashioning and affirming a new aesthetic.[2] At a distance of thirty or forty years it seems an era when new literary and artistic movements were born almost yearly, when each new "little magazine" brought forth a new "ism." When the magazine, as happened often enough, ceased publication after a few numbers, its writers and editors might soon reappear in the pages of still another one. Much debate was devoted to defining the differences between one tendency and another, and the literary rivalries and friendships of the period were frequently enlivened by a theatrical and apocalyptic tone. For each new "ism" sought to lay to rest all the others; each new movement sought to prove conclusively that it alone knew the path future art must follow.[3]

The period from 1920 to 1935 was one in which the major figures of the Generation of 1898, Azorín, Baroja, Antonio Machado, Unamuno, and Valle-Inclán were still producing important works. Novels and poetry of note were also being written by Juan Ramón Jiménez, Pérez de Ayala and Gómez de la Serna. In these years as well, the essay had begun to attract a wide number of important talents. In addition to Ortega y Gasset, who had begun writing in the preceding decade, this period saw the production of notable contributions to the essay by José María de Cossío,

Melchor Fernández Almagro, José Gaos, Ernesto Giménez Caballero, Antonio Marichalar, Gregorio Marañón, Adolfo Salazar, and Fernando Vela.

But it is perhaps with the poets who came to prominence in these years that we find the most varied and profound literary talents, talents influential both in Spain and abroad. This group, sometimes referred to as the Generation of the [Primo de Rivera] Dictatorship,[4] consisted of the following poets: Rafael Alberti, Vicente Aleixandre, Dámaso Alonso, Manuel Altolaguirre, Luis Cernuda, Gerardo Diego, Juan José Domenchina, León Felipe, Federico García Lorca, Pedro Garfias, Jorge Guillén, José Moreno Villa, Emilio Prados, and Pedro Salinas. It is beyond the scope of this book to deal with the diversity of the Generation's poetic output. It must suffice to point to its importance in comprising an infusion of new life into Spanish poetry. Aware of and open to the latest poetic production of Europe and America, by temperament innovative and even iconoclastic, the group as a whole aimed at the creation of new interpretation of reality, one which would raise reality to a higher level.[5] The prose writers, especially the novelists of the Generation of 1927, shared with the poets an urge toward the new and innovative, an urge to reinterpret Spanish reality, and to forge a new expressive language as the vehicle for their reinterpretation.

Jarnés, one of the older members of the Generation of 1927, reflected the innovative spirit of those in the vanguard. In his essays and book reviews, he put forth the most clear-cut statement of the novelist's need to move in new directions which is to be found in the 1930's in Spain. As we shall see below, his views summarized and made concrete those of Ortega y Gasset for whose judgment in aesthetic matters Jarnés often expressed admiration.[6] Over the nine-year period between 1927 and 1936, Jarnés expressed his concept of the novel in terms nearly identical to those of Ortega.

Concerning the novel's function, he wrote: "It is not always creative to introduce into the novel some men everyone knows, and it's puerile Futurist hocus-pocus to introduce men whom no one can know. So much for Balzac and Wells. To strip the character of that skin which can be reproduced by a Kodak or the news pages, and endow him with another skin . . . which can be developed on the artist's sensitive plates, this is, perhaps, the function of the novel. . . . The novel is the expression of a life which cannot be completely lived" (*Rúbricas* [*Flourishes*], p. 148).

One way of achieving the vision of a life which is not completely realistic is to see the world with fresh eyes, the eyes of a child. "The most beautiful book will be the one in which a child tells us about his first astonishment at the glimpses of things, of his first stirring before naked beauty. Those books are always written by old men, and between childhood and old age, there are many walls of glass which erase pure perspective or make it irridescent" (*Ejercicios* [*Exercises*], p. 58). Jarnés places a high value on innovation, and on a fresh vision of the world. But where the same concern in, for example, the Surrealists leads them to choose a new subject matter, the workings of the unconscious mind (while retaining traditional techniques of art), Jarnés' concern leads him to choose a new style of looking (while retaining traditional subject matter). In 1929, Jarnés repeated the idea: "It will be necessary for us to fall in love with the world again, merrily, like children. We should be intimate with it. Be disrespectful. Pull its mane as we would a tame lion's."[7] This is perhaps the only Romantic aspect of his aesthetic, an aspect which has its roots in the belief that the child, the innocent, or the "noble savage," perceives the purest reality and has the most valid vision of life.

This Romantic aspect reaches its maximum development in Jarnés' view of the novelist as a kind of prophet, possessed of lyrical gifts which enable him to transform everyday reality into art. "The novelist ought always be a travelling poet. Like every traveller, he will tire, he will sit down to rest, he will forget a little the wingèd Hermes who guides him; but, hanging from his belt he will always carry his flask of generous lyric wine. One swallow will suffice to cure him of his fatigue" (*ibid.*, p. 75). Since the novelist is no longer to be an objective observer of lived reality, he will not produce a prosaic novel. His will be rather a lyrical one.

The novel, according to Jarnés, had become poetic; thus each novel is individual, unique. Jarnés wrote, à propos of Dostoevsky: "Dostoiewski is unique. Each novel of his produces this impression of singularity on us. The characters of all his novels might be brothers, might reveal themselves in identical gestures;

but their life trajectories are new in each book, and to follow them always makes us approach unknown vistas" (*Flourishes*, p. 166). The uniqueness he saw in Dostoevsky was one of the things that led Jarnés to postulate singularity as the primary goal in the novel. Where Ortega had tended to consider the Romantic-Naturalist novel as *the* novel, Jarnés admitted into the genre many other types of novel.

Echoing Ortega's remark to the effect that "In art repetition is invalid," Jarnés remarks that the author's "inescapable mission is to differentiate himself, to create a personal world; otherwise, he is insignificant, he doesn't signify, he's not an author, only a writer, or perhaps a parasite, or a dealer in previous literatures which are easy to simulate."[8] Here, it seems, Jarnés believed that the author can create a personal world, and further, that he knows himself sufficiently well to know his own personal world.

Of course, an implicit assumption here is that in the quest for self-knowledge the artist will discover something unique. The haunting and depressing possibility that one's self might turn out to be like others' selves does not seem to have concerned Jarnés to the extent that it has some Existentialists.

With Galdós, and the Realist novel, there had been no question of the personal world, for the novelist's task was to describe the external world which was accessible to everyone. With Unamuno, and other novelists of the Generation of 1898, except perhaps Baroja, the novel could be a personal world, but the emphasis lay on the personality of and in that world, rather than on its worldiness. That is, Unamuno believed that self-knowledge was problematical; his writings were attempts to discover whether he could know himself. When Jarnés assumes that the novelist already knows himself, the emphasis falls upon the literary expression and aritistic execution of the personal world which he has discovered, which he knows.

In what may well have been a reaction against Unamuno's novels, Jarnés thought the novelist ought not content himself with presenting his own memories or his own "unrestrainable impulses" (*Flourishes*, p. 30). The necessity for invention is obvious if the novelist is to be more than a mere recorder of facts or of autobiographical details. In restraining the autobiographical and anecdotal element, Jarnés not only implies that his own personal experiences are not inherently worthy of artistic treatment, but also that the experiences of other men, the ordinary man, the mass-man, are equally unworthy. He implies that "anyone" can have experiences, but that what makes them suitable material for a novel is the artistic skill with which the writer shapes them to make them fit into a novel. We need hardly emphasize that this point of view is quite opposed to the post-war importance attached to the testimonial value of the experiences of the writer. Perhaps the shift to a greater stress on the testimonial function of literature responds to the increasing impact of Existentialism, perhaps to changes in the function of media other than literature, perhaps to the widely held notion that what a person experiences is important *because* he experiences it, not because the experience itself is essentially meaningful.

The concept of the novel centers, then, on a special view of what is novelisable. Everyday life is suitable material for Jarnés' novel only after it has been transformed into poetry by the sensitivity and sensibility of the novelist. Too much individualization of this sensitivity leads to incomprehensibility. Too little leads to a lack of art in the novel. A fine balance is sought between the exterior data, what are found, and the interior data, what are invented. Salazar y Chapela, having discussed the question, described Jarnés' first novel quite accurately: "We have said that the Useless Professor's world, through which he slips smilingly, is a 'smooth, flat, colorful, agreeable, attractive' world. . . . But we have to mention that not on that account is Benjamín Jarnés' 'literary planimetry' absolute at all. Behind this smooth, beautiful surface, with no reticence, of the *Useless Professor,* we notice a texture of emotions, ideas and feelings."[9]

Because Jarnés' novel is unique, individualized and emphatically stylistic in character, it requires an audience which is somewhat specialized. The "common reader" finds this novel impenetrable, or irreparably flawed. "Now, the great mass of readers comes to the mass-writer who writes 'plainly,' that is, with no distinction, and at first feels the fulfillment of meeting an equal, then the gratitude which demands a subject resigned to sacrificing his individuality to write in the style common to his reader" (*Exercises,* p. 22). The Orteguian disdain for the "mass" of readers makes its appearance in Jarnés. If the novel is indeed an "aristocracy of the poem" then it requires an aristocratic audience for its appreciation.

The common language of the common reader is too restricted

for Jarnés. It is not poetic enough. "Every idiom is a certain petrification of the language; and it's usually the parlance of common sense" (*ibid.*, p. 16). Jarnés objects to the ready-made phrase, just as Unamuno had done. The latter's objection was based on the necessity for invention in order to express his individual and unique personality. The former's objection is grounded on the necessity for invention in order to create poetry.[10] Set forms of any kind are unacceptable because they are non- or anti-poetic. "I think that the return to the strophe is the return of the defeated. The bird returns to the cage when he doesn't know what to do with his wings" (*ibid.*, p. 85).[11]

The flight from the restrictions of the ready-made phrase, or the ready-made form, leads to the creation of poetry and style. "Style is something which floats on top of all the easy prescriptions. . . . Style is, perhaps, a peculiar condition which is revealed in each moment of the work. When a work has not been *stylized* it means it has not been produced by that peculiar aesthetic condition, but in a moment of abandon, or of excessive technical virtuosity. To stylize a page is to create it in our very own image, the only way to create. In literature—as in all art—either one makes style or one is unnecessary."[12] Jarnés is in the somewhat ambiguous position of affirming, as did the Romantics, the necessity for an individualized vision of reality, and of denying, as they did not, the spontaneous expression of this vision. Thus, although Jarnés is allied to the Romantic tradition in regard to the subject matter of the novel, he is opposed to it in regard to the expression of the subject matter.

It is interesting in this connection to recall a comment of Ortega's: "The moment we are sincere the gorilla will rise up within us and claim his peremptory rights: only by dint of fictions and fantasies will we keep him chained up. Romanticism, Anarchism, Energumenism are perhaps no more than attempts to justify the weakness of the man who is struggling with his internal orangutan."[13] Implicit in this view is the belief that a lack of restraint is a sign of weakness. Here, we think Ortega is oversimplifying the matter. For the expression of sincerity may indicate, instead of an inability to restrain oneself, merely the desire not to. Further, in a larger context, Ortega's comments indicate that the expression of sincerity is somehow easier than its restraint. This accords well with his notion of art as a difficult activity capable of being mastered only by those with special qualifications. Jarnés shared Ortega's view of the need for discipline in art and in the novelist.

There is an additional aspect to Ortega's remarks which needs to be commented upon. The "internal orangutan" needs to be suppressed. Art should not confront the individual in his intimate, real-life concerns, nor should it be the expression of those concerns in the author. Essentially, Ortega is arguing for the suppression of the "thesis" in a work of art. To the extent that he urges the suppression of the "thesis" he is assuming a position in line with those critics of the nineteenth century in Spain, of whom Menéndez y Pelayo is the most prominent example, who criticized Galdós' novels because they contained a "thesis."

Criticism from Galdós' day to this has tended to view the novel and its "thesis" as separable entitles. One school holds that the novel should contain no thesis; the other that it should, or at least that it is not an inferior novel merely because it does. In our view, the central issue of the debate over the novel which took place in the late 1920's and the 1930's was precisely the admissibility of a "thesis" into the novel. We shall examine some of the salient aspects of this issue in their relation to Jarnés' aesthetic.

The novel is always a representation of life. There are many reasons why this is so, perhaps the fundamental one being that the novel is always a product of a human mind which has been acted upon by experience. The novelist has only two tools with which to work: himself, and his language. The novelist may use much or little of his experience, portraying it faithfully (i.e., in true-to-life fashion) or distorting it. The novelist may, to record his experiences, employ either a primarily common language or a mostly individual one. His common language is the one most easily understood by the majority of the literate public. Galdós' language provided no problem for his readers for the most part, because it was the language they spoke every day. At the other extreme, the novelist may use a highly stylized language—and as Jarnés points out, a style is always individual—or even his own idiolect. In this case the reader may encounter considerable difficulty in understanding the novel.

The novelist's language is always related to his experience. He learns his language because he needs to deal with the real world.

He may attempt to reorder, or distort this real world by reordering his language; e.g., he may shun the ready-made phrase, the idiom, as does Jarnés, in order to create new verbal combinations. It is taken for granted that there are referents in the real world of experience for any of the language which a literary artist uses. Only when the artist attempts to record his experience by non-verbal means does it become impossible to discover the referents. But in this case, he would not produce a novel, but a painting or a sonata.

Many factors have combined to make the novelist's interpretation of life seem more important than it did formerly. Romanticism's emphasis on the individual personality of the author, and the validity and value of his perceptions, is a prime influence. Naturalism's emphasis on "real life" problems, and its attempt to make the novel scientifically experimental, is another. The view of "art for art's sake" has become somewhat discredited under the influence of Existentialism and its demand that the writer be *engagé*, although not necessarily in the political or social sense. If he were not *engagé*, if he were not moved or impelled to write by pressing personal concerns, he would not have written. This implies that every novel, by attempting to interpret life or a portion of life's meaning, relies upon a preexistent interpretive view of life.

The interpretive system is analogous to a metalanguage which linguists use to speak about natural languages. And just as a metalanguage is not a language in the common sense, an interpretive system of life is not life. But by conditioning the nature of the novel, determining what it shall include and how this shall be structured, the interpretive system of the novelist has an existence of its own, and can be discussed separately from any given novel. We usually can call this system the *Weltanschauung* of the novelist. And it is this system which constitutes the "thesis" of very nearly every novel. Indeed, so far as we know, no novel can exist without it, and to this extent, every novel is a thesis novel. Thus, it is not the subject matter *per se* which constitutes the thesis and which is objectionable. It is the obtrusive quality of the subject matter which offends.

Those critics who object to the "thesis" novel would likely agree with Baquero Goyanes when he says that "the novel . . . seems to us like a genre always in service of the revolutionary forces, enemies of established society."[14] But if this is true, it is true only in a special sense. The great innovators in the novel must always seem revolutionary, even revolutionary in politics at times, for the simple reason that innovation means a departure from the accepted norms. It means the creation of new norms. To constrain the novelist to the production of novels of a given type is to stifle his innovative gifts. And it seems that if the genre is to flower from generation to generation, to grow and mature, it must be nourished by the innovations of the great novelists, even when these are "revolutionary."

We must remember, further, that not all innovation is revolutionary, for this quality depends not upon the novel but upon the interpretive system of the novelist. Thus, we could hardly call the novels of Gabriel Miró revolutionary in Baquero's sense, although they were clearly innovative as novels. It might almost be taken as axiomatic that the great novel is by definition the one which departs from norms accepted prior to its appearance. Every great novel is almost a novel *sui generis*. Curiously enough, Unamuno expressed a view directly opposed to that of Baquero, in a letter to Giménez Caballero, long-time friend of Jarnés, dated March 16, 1927. He denounced "those vanguard literatures which almost always mask a politics—that most holy word which makes a religion of ethics—of conservatism."[15] In view of Ortega's opinion of art as a mysterious object to be approached only by the sensitive, and of Jarnés' view of the novel as an "aristocracy of the poem"—that is, of the elitist tendencies of the vanguard movements in general—Unamuno's statement is directly pertinent.

As the notion of "art for art's sake" has gradually lost credit, the idea that art should adhere more closely to real life has become more widely accepted. The tendency toward increasing realism, both in the depiction of external reality and of the author's inner vision, his sincerity, has had the effect of putting the novel more in touch with the age which produced it. One result of the increasingly close relation between the novel and its lived context is that novels which are very "timely" become dated easily. While this is particularly true of topical novels which are usually written under the stimulus of some particular historical or social event, it is also true to a lesser extent of the thesis novel in general. For example, the opinion we so often hear from literary critics that *Don Quixote* (or *Hamlet* or *Faust*) is a timeless work is based on the view that the "thesis" it contains is not a topical one, not a timely one, but rather one which deals with eternal aspects of man's condition.

II   *The Influence of Ortega y Gasset*

The philosopher José Ortega y Gasset played a crucial role in the formulation of the novelistic theory of the Generation of 1927. His interest in and writings on literature are well known and we doubt that Jarnés would have held the view of the novel he did had he not known Ortega's essays on the subject. The two works which will concern us in particular here, *La deshumanización del arte (The Dehumanization of Art)*, and *Ideas sobre la novela (Ideas on the Novel)*, have been and will likely continue to be a source of much discussion, for they set forth one of the two major theoretical positions on the nature and function of art and literature which became generalized in Spain and Europe in the first third of this century.

Ortega's thinking on literature had an extraordinary effect on a large number of Spanish writers and intellectuals. To them, Ortega represented, first of all, a living refutation of that part of the Black Legend which argued that Spain was culturally backward with regard to Europe, unable to produce philosophers, scientists, and writers of universal appeal and high calibre.[16] Rosa Chacel recalled Ortega's influence upon his students and friends as that of the model intellectual.[17]

Although Ortega and those who were his disciples took a strong stand against what they considered the limitations of Spanish culture, e.g., its parochialism, isolation from Europe, lack of a strong tradition of intellectual rigor and discipline, they did not often grapple with such limitations by criticizing everyday events. Rather their criticism reached a fairly abstract plane which seemed not to concern itself with daily practicalities.[18] One reason for this was Ortega's role as a philosopher; while he considered nothing to be "off-limits" to his analytical and critical attention, his approach tended toward the theoretical or abstract rather than the practical. Another reason may have been, as Ayala suggests, an atmosphere of waiting during the dictatorship of Primo de Rivera. Even if Primo's government could be called a *dictablanda*—to borrow a term from some of the more easy-going critics of Franco's regime—the fact remains that it did exile Unamuno and, in 1930, imprison Valle-Inclán.

We are not suggesting political timidity on the part of Ortega's group, but rather their belief that direct involvement in practical politics was either unworthy of or unfruitful for them. The role of politician was all too likely to be associated in the minds of the Generation with the futile rotation in office of opposing parties, like that which characterized a good part of Spanish political life in the nineteenth century, or with a venerable tradition of political oratory uniformly denounced for its emptiness and rhetorical paroxysms.

In examining Ortega's statements on the art of the novel, we shall often find that his remarks lend themselves to interpretations of a political and social sort. His view of art as a privileged occupation was particularly open to criticism along social lines.

An early statement on Proust, which appeared in the Proust homage volume of *La Nouvelle Revue Française* in 1923, foreshadows the more extended formulations which Ortega published in 1925. The first major point Ortega makes in his article on Proust is that the subject of a work of art is never particularly important nor very revealing of the nature of the individual artist. "The important thing for them [Claude Monet and Edgar Degas], the motive force of their canvases, is ethereal perspective, the fabric of chromatic vibrations in which things, whatever they are, are enveloped and exist sumptuously."[10] It would seem that this assertion holds good when themes of paintings are examined within chronological periods. Each movement in art seems to take a certain limited area of subject matter for its domain. In the twentieth century, for example, the analytical Cubist period in painting is defined by the fact that it restricted its subject matter almost entirely to still lifes. When other subjects such as human figures began to appear (e.g., in Marcel Duchamp's "Nude Descending a Staircase," 1912, and Ferdinand Léger's "Soldier With a Pipe," 1916), the analytical stage of Cubism is considered to have been drawing to a close and the synthetic stage to be beginning.

It seems that each period establishes, by its reaction to former ones, its own special province. Those working within a given artistic school during a given period tend to exploit this province as fully as possible. Soon or late, the province seems to have been fully explored, and a new group announces its reaction to its predecessors, and delimits new provinces.

There are many difficulties in trying to extend to fiction critical categories which arise in other art forms. However, Ortega's view is apt enough when applied to the Impressionist painters. Their primary concern, as was true of the Cubists who followed and reacted against them, was one of technique. Where the Impressionists attempted to blur the hard outlines of things, the Cubists tried to multiply these outlines by painting the object as if it were viewed simultaneously from several points of view.

Regarding the Impressionists' blurring of outlines, Ortega wrote that the pointillist technique allowed the object on the canvas, itself unformed and without a sharp outline, to take shape as a vibrating presence before the viewer's "half-closed eyes" (ibid., p. 272). These remarks which resemble those he made in Meditaciones del Quijote (Meditations on the Quixote), and in "Sobre la caza" ("On Hunting,"), 1943, continue the sense of Ortega's famous phrase: Yo soy yo y mi circunstancia ("I am myself and my situation"). For if it is true that objects do not have sharp outlines which set them off from their surroundings, then it is also true that the object must be considered in conjunction with its context.

In regard to Proust, Ortega asserts a similar concern as that which the Impressionist painters displayed. "In sum, Proust brings to literature what one could call a general atmospheric intention. Landscapes and men, the exterior world and the interior world, everything in him evaporates in an airy and diffuse palpitation" (ibid., p. 275).

Proust's achievement, in Ortega's opinion, depends also upon his handling of time. Just as objects in space lose their outlines and the interior world is fused with the exterior one, so moments in time lose their integrity. Proust's fictional method, perhaps an elaboration of Bergson's concept of "la durée," had the effect of erasing the boundaries of distinct moments in time. Ortega felt that the impact of such a procedure on the reader was a sort of torture: "The fact is that Proust's muse could be called 'laggardly' and his style consists of the literary exploitation of that delectatio morosa which the Councils have so severely punished" (ibid., p. 278). Innovation, then, in the handling of space and time constitute Proust's achievement in fiction.

When we turn to The Dehumanization of Art (1925) we are

not surprised to find emphasized the aspect of innovation in the arts. "Each style which appears in History can give rise to a certain number of different forms within a generic type. But the day comes when the marvelous pitcher is empty. This has happened, for example, with the novel and the Romantic-Naturalist theater. It is a naive mistake to think that the present sterility of both genres is due to the absence of talented people. What happens is that within them [the genres] all the possible combinations have been exhausted."[20]

These remarks point to the fact that artistic styles indeed seem to possess an ebb and flow, rushing uniformly into any new channel which has been opened, filling it, and then receding to seek a new channel. The channels of artistic innovation are opened by the pioneering work of the creator within a genre. Once Galdós had opened the channel of the Realist-Naturalist novel in Spain, it became filled with works by authors such as Palacio Valdés, Blasco Ibáñez, Ricardo León, and others, which were, by dint of their lack of innovation in form or content, generally unoriginal. By 1925, this genre had lost all possibility, in Ortega's view, of extension; it was exhausted. A new channel needed to be opened. This was to be accomplished for Spain as well as for the rest of Western Europe, by what Ortega called the process of "dehumanization."

Ortega, responding to quite obvious developments in European art, labelled dehumanization that general tendency to dispense with recognizable human forms in painting. This dehumanized channel was opened by Picasso and Cubism. It extends through Surrealism until the present day when it manifests itself as Abstract Expressionism and Op Art. There was no question in Ortega's mind of the necessity of some relationship between the work of art and the real world all men live in. As he remarks: "A painting, a poem in which there were no remnant of experienced forms, would be unintelligible; that is, they would not be anything, just as a speech in which each word had been stripped of its usual meaning" (*ibid.*, p. 363). That is, the completely autistic production cannot be a work of art, cannot be anything, because one cannot gauge the artistry by reference to anything in one's life.

Ortega offers several reasons for the vogue of dehumanized art. He sees it as a result of negative temperament, an "aggressive-

ness and mocking of old art" (*ibid.*, p. 379). He mentions the
artist's antipathy to traditional interpretations, of reality (*ibid.*,
p. 380). In addition, he realized that the artist's task is essentially
to deform reality, to make it conform to his own private vision
of the real world (*ibid.*, p. 365). Art's justification lies in its
innovation; it cannot justify itself if "it limits itself to reproducing
reality, duplicating it in vain. Its mission is to evoke an unreal
horizon. To achieve this there is no other means than to deny
our reality, placing ourselves by this act above it. To be an
artist is not to take seriously that serious man we are when we are
not artists" (*ibid.*, p. 382). The view of the artist as hero has its
roots in this attitude. The artist's refusal to accept his lived
reality as material for his art is essentially, according to Ortega,
an heroic stance. Jarnés was to appropriate these ideas completely, and give special weight to the necessary lack of seriousness of the artist; Jarnés extended and elaborated Ortega's notion
into a complex theory of the need for humor in art.

In his *Ideas sobre la novela (Ideas on the Novel)*, Ortega
expands upon some of the points he made in *The Dehumanization
of Art*. He asserts the exhaustion of the novelistic genre, and
says this is due to a lack of new themes. "It's practically impossible to find new themes. This is the first factor in the enormous
objective, not personal, difficulty which is implied by composing
a novel in our day and age."[21] The crisis which Ortega saw
arising out of what he thought was the impossibility of finding
new themes owed its urgency to Ortega's belief in the need for
art to be innovative. Eleven years previously he had written:
"Every real poet, whether prolific or of scanty output, is . . .
irreplaceable. A scientist is superseded by another who follows
him: a poet is always literarily insurmountable. On the other
hand, every imitation in art is obviously unsuitable. What for?
In science precisely that which can be repeated is valuable; but
style is always an only child."[22]

Ortega expresses his belief that what is important in a novel
is not the theme, or the plot, but rather the manner in which the
novel is written. "In its beginnings one could believe that what
is important for the novel is its plot. Later one has come to notice
that what is important is not *what* is seen, but *that* something
human, whatever it be, be seen clearly" (*Ideas on the Novel*,
p. 392). This position emphasizes drama rather than painting in

the novelist's presentation of his fictional materials.[23] The reason for this is that the reader is forced to participate in the novel if the novelist merely describes. "If I read in a novel: 'Peter is splenetic,' it's as if the author were inviting me to create in my fantasy the spleen of Peter, taking off from his definition. That is, that he obliges me to be a novelist" *(loc. cit.).*

We should note the gulf between the Ortega-Jarnés view of this question and a view which has become widespread in recent years. In the works of Cortázar, Robbe-Grillet, Fuentes, and others, a very specific demand is made upon the reader that he become, in some measure, the novelist. Not only is the reader urged to recreate in his fantasy the traits of the characters, but he is also invited and sometimes forced to reconstruct in his mind the very structure of the novel.

On the one hand, Ortega is censuring the novelist who elicits an active response in the reader. On the other, he is censuring the one who merely describes the characters, without "presenting" them. We recognize this as one source of Ortega's antipathy to the novels of Unamuno, for Unamuno's avowed aim was for the reader to be the novelist. Unamuno's view was partly based on his recognition that elements of fantasy and identification are central to the reader's response to the novel. Unamuno wanted the reader of *La tía Tula* to acknowledge his own feelings of maternity, as one step in the process of creating and recreating Gertrudis as a character. He encouraged this identification on the part of the reader. It is precisely these elements of reader response which Ortega censures, because he deems them anti-aesthetic.

Although, according to Ortega, the novelist should present the characters in action, this does not mean that the novel should consist entirely or mostly of action. Ortega says that it is an error to attribute the reader's boredom with a novel to a plot which is "not very interesting" (*ibid.,* p. 393). For what takes place in the novel is not what interests the reader. The characters do interest him, and therefore, anything they do is important and interesting (*ibid.,* p. 394). The solution to the problem posed by the absence of suitable plots or themes is to invent interesting characters whose actions, because performed by them, will be interesting. "For I suspect that the serious novel today must turn from [adventures] to [characters] and rather than invent plots interesting in themselves—which is practically impossible—think up attractive people" (*ibid.*, p. 398).

At this point, Lubbock's terms are not adequate to encompass Ortega's distinction. While Ortega initially appears to follow these terms, arguing as does Lubbock that "drama" is more vivid or more effective than "picture" in the novel, he later draws another distinction which Lubbock does not. Ortega distinguishes between "drama" as plot-action, and "drama" as individuals in action. This shift in emphasis corresponds to that noted by E. M. Forster in his separation of "story" from "plot" in a novel.[24]

In predicting that the novel would have to turn to "characters" or to an emphasis on "plot" in Forster's terms, Ortega is predicting the advent of the "psychological" novel of the sort which exploits the characters' unconscious lives. At the time Ortega wrote this, Joyce's *Ulysses,* a novel which fits Ortega's description perhaps as well as any, had been in print for four years.

Although in certain ways Jarnés' novels are psychological within the meaning Ortega intended, they were not psychological in the Joycean or Kafkaesque sense. In Jarnés' characters we are basically in the realm of cognitive psychology, the psychology of vision, audition, and sensation. Because of our author's hostility to Freudian, indeed to all depth, psychology, his novels lack any of the psychology of the irrational which marks so much of twentieth-century fiction. Unlike Unamuno, for whose literary gifts he felt some affinity, Jarnés never portrayed any of the nuclear situations so prominent in the research of the depth psychologists. Nowhere in his work do we find instances of incest, sibling rivalry, homicidal impulses directed toward a parent or a child. Nor did Jarnés make use of the interior monologue; his characters' monologues are the ruminations of their conscious minds. We do not find in Jarnés' novels the cathected symbols so frequent in Joyce, e.g., the house keys of Leopold Bloom or the top hat of Molly Bloom's lover, Blazes Boylan, whose peregrinations in *Ulysses* provide a leitmotif and a key to understanding Bloom's actions in the novel.

The novel, then, must describe or invent "interesting people." However, it must do this without confronting the reader's real-life concerns: "The author's tactic must consist in isolating the reader from his real surroundings and imprisoning him in a little hermetic and imaginary environment which is the interior world of the novel. In a word, he must *populate* it, get us to be interested in the people he presents who, even though they were most admirable, would not collide with the flesh and blood beings who surround the reader and constantly demand his interest. Make of the reader a passing 'visitor from the provinces'; this is, to my way of thinking, the great secret of the novelist" (*ibid.*, p. 409). The world of the novel must be hermetic, self-contained, without reference to real-life problems. The novelist may be "as Realistic as you like, that is, his novelistic microcosm may be made with the most real of materials; but when we are inside it, let us not miss anything of what is real which was left outside. This is the reason for which every novel laden with transcendental intentions, be they political, ideological, symbolic or satirical, is stillborn" (*ibid.*, p. 411).

The insistence that the novel be a self-contained world, detached from common lived reality is perhaps an exaggeration of Ortega's views on art.[25] He felt that the work of art was somehow set apart from real life. It contained mysteries and secrets which could only be appreciated or apprehended by a rather small group of sensitive individuals, the initiates. He was dismayed by the fact that the "Romantic-Naturalist" novel and theater were capable of being understood by anyone, by the average reader. He saw this as the debasement of art. His view of art as something separate from and distant from real life can be seen in his comments on the beauty of a drinking glass. He says that if offered a glass of water when thirsty, he does not want to contemplate the beauty of the design of the glass. "Either I attend to the slaking of my thirst or I attend to Beauty: any middle ground would be the falsification of both things. When I am thirsty, please, give me a full glass, clean and without beauty."[26]

Essentially this view represents Ortega's idealism, and also his disinclination to compromise. For the glass of beautiful design erases the boundaries between the utilitarian glass and the *objet d'art*. It is a mixed form, just as the prose poem, or the novel-in-dialogue. The breaking down of categories which is inherent in any mixed form was distasteful to Ortega.

Consistent with Ortega's view of art as a mysterious world of beauty, a cult of beauty, is his belief that the young writer must think seriously about the "crisis" of the novel before he could produce a worthwhile novel. "But I doubt that [young writers] will find the trail of such secret and profound veins if before they start to write their novels they do not feel, for a long while, terror. From someone who has not perceived the grave hour which today haunts this genre nothing can be expected" (*Ideas on the Novel*, p. 419). Ortega would have the novelist be "classical" in his technique; i.e., he would have him control the creative process consciously. He should renounce the spontaneous, "inspired" novel which the Romantics produced.

The controversial nature of Ortega's *Ideas on the Novel* gave rise to a polemic over the nature of the novel. Perhaps the most famous writer to take issue with Ortega was Pío Baroja. In a prologue written in 1925 for his novel *La nave de los locos (The Ship of Fools)*, Baroja disagreed with Ortega in terms which are valuable for the way in which they foreshadow the later criticism of Ortega's views, and for the light they shed on the status of the novel as a genre in the 1920s and 1930s.

Baroja first disagrees with Ortega's opinion that the novel must be a world unto itself. "If closing the novel to the outside air constituted a great merit, all or almost all the Spanish novelists of the nineteenth century would be admirable. The majority had a great enthusiasm for the limited and closed."[27] Baroja's opinion is that the novel should be in touch with real life.

Secondly, Baroja disputed Ortega's view of the novel as a genre with a unified form. He thought the novel was "a multiform genre, protean, still being formed" (*ibid.*, p. 313). His attack on Ortega takes shape on this point, for he says that anyone who thinks the immense variety of the novel can fit a single mold is being doctrinaire and dogmatic. Where Ortega saw the "hermetic" novel as more difficult to write, Baroja felt it was easier. To do other than draw upon real life was to create a novel which was dry and dead.

Thirdly, Baroja supports the necessity of "ideas" in the novel. He believes that the novel which focusses on a few interesting characters, and which has only the bit of drama called for by Ortega, is too rhetorical. "The novelist who writes a thick book with few characters does it on rhetoric, which is another form of writer's erudition. The heaviness, laggardliness, the slow rhythm cannot be virtues. Laggardliness is antibiological and antivital" (*ibid.*, p. 321). Curiously, this was exactly the position

Ortega had taken in his article on Proust. Evidently, Ortega's view changed somewhat between the publication of that article in 1923, and the appearance of the *Ideas on the Novel* in 1925. For in the latter work, no mention is made of the difficulty a reader encounters with the *novela morosa*. In the latter work, Ortega seems to invite this difficulty, for it is one means of distancing the novel from the common, insensitive reader, and restoring it to its place of high honor as a work of art.

Although Baroja's comments are quite aggressive, it should be remembered that Ortega invited criticism or rectification of his ideas. His closing remarks to the *Ideas on the Novel* indicate this: "I repeat that with them [these thoughts on the novel] I do not pretend to instruct those who know more about these things than I. It is possible that everything I've said is completely mistaken. It doesn't matter at all if it has served to incite a few young writers, seriously concerned about their art, to undertake to explore the difficult and subterranean possibilities which are still left to the ancient destiny of the novel" *(Ideas on the Novel,* p. 419). Ortega's professed willingness to have his ideas rectified by others has been ignored or misunderstood. As Jarnés and others knew, Ortega's views were descriptive, not prescriptive.[28] Yet, a commentator forty years later still thought that Ortega was trying to justify dehumanized art.[29] His thinking did indeed incite younger writers to think through the assumptions underlying their production in the genre.

II *Limitations of the Jarnesian Aesthetic*

There are many reasons why Jarnés' theory of the novel, inspired as it was by Ortega's view of modern art, has proved to be substantially an unworkable one. Under the impetus of Ortega's efforts to bring to Spain the current thinking in European philosophy and art, Jarnés and his generation chose not to follow the path set out by the Generation of 1898, essentially a path of self-investigation, the search for their own and Spain's unique personality and historical reality.

The Generation of 1927 felt that its task was to restore to the novel the artistry it had lost because of the emphasis of the previous Generation on subject matter and the personal voice of the author. The Generation of 1927 proposed to dispense in large measure with the subject matter, and to control the personal voice of the author. Rosa Chacel writes: "The Spaniard had got the nineteenth century stuck in his throat, the century of the novel, a democratic art, with which he only managed to make a clumsy art, in ninety-nine percent of the cases. So, we had no image of our immediate past which was sufficiently noble—*literarily* noble, you understand—we had to begin by trying our wings, in drawing simple profiles, in which the line, that is, the mode of speech, was pure, and what was depicted, that is, the theme, was commonplace, the everyday, aesthetically safe."[30]

This Generation rejected the interpretation of Spanish reality which had been given by the preceding generation because it was insufficiently noble.[31] They felt it necessary to begin again the interpretation of Spanish reality; the first step toward this goal was the one of creating a generational idiom, a verbal style adequate to the generation and its concerns. Jarnés' generation —and let us not forget the prominence in it of the poetic talents of Lorca, Salinas, and Guillén—attempted to forge an artistic, poetic style, as the first step toward their reinterpretation of Spanish reality.

The will to style dominated the concerns of the generation. It led them to neglect the lived reality which surrounded them. And while Ortega's thinking seemed to justify such neglect, in the novel at least, it also argued for unification of the external world (i.e., of subject matter) with the internal world (i.e., of style) in his phrase: *Yo soy yo y mi circunstancia.* Below, we shall show how Jarnés strove to effect this unification. But for the most part, for the novel at least, the attempt had little success. The generation's neglect of the objective, lived context, of their *circunstancia,* appears to readers in the 1940's and after as a rejection of it. Where the novelists attended to the concrete reality around them—as Jarnés did the rural and urban landscapes in *Paula y Paulita, (Paula and Paulette)* and *Lo rojo y lo azul (The Red and the Blue)*—they did so for the purpose of transforming it aesthetically, not for the purpose of reforming it ethically.[32]

The Generation's dispensing with their real life surroundings implies a rejection of them, it is true; however, they did not go so far as earlier writers (e.g. the Romantics) and choose exotic themes, Oriental or African. Where Africa is mentioned at all in their works, it is the North Africa of the disastrous Moroccan War in the 1920's (as in José Díaz Fernández' *El blocao* [1928], and Jarnés' *The Red and the Blue*) and not an Africa full of adventurous possibilities as in Ganivet's *La conquista del reino de Maya por el último conquistador español, Pío Cid* (1897). Those who were closest to Jarnés' aesthetic position found themselves in a distasteful environment, but did not reject it stringently; instead they attempted to reveal its poetic aspects to show that it was not the distasteful environment that it seemed. Between rejection and renovation there is a considerable difference. As Unamuno saw it, the Generation had substituted the means of literature (language and style) for its end (the interpretation of life). A large portion of the criticism which has been directed at Jarnés and his literary method stems from some point of view which usually holds that there is a single purpose or province for the novel. Such a point of view fails to take account of the formlessness of the genre and its lack of stylistic norms. McLuhan put the matter quite well when he said: "The difference between the artist and the organization man in these matters [the influence of radio and film on literature] would seem to be that the artist senses at once the creative possibilities in new media even when they are alien to his own medium. Whereas the bureaucrat of arts and letters moans and bristles whenever the museum of exhibits is threatened by invasion or desertion. The artist is the historian of the future because he uses the unnoticed possibilities of the present."[33] Indeed, those poetic possibilities exploited by Jarnés have had their impact on more recent novels, not necessarily through his direct influence, but rather because of the general influence of his generation both within and outside of Spain.

Jarnés' novels are, like those of the other members of the Generation, essays in style and technique. Backed by the formulations of Ortega, Jarnés developed a concept of the novel as style. In this, he joined Gabriel Miró and Gómez de la Serna who were emphasizing style in the novel. His achievement is directly in line with that of Joyce and Proust, although of lesser magnitude. For by concentrating on style, Jarnés' novels do provide an interpretation of reality.

Although Jarnés has been criticized for an excessive emphasis on style, it was clearly not his intention to destroy reality, i.e., subject matter. For in a revealing passage, he asserts the necessity for a unity between style and content: "We can recognize the bad novelist in *his settings*—as he calls them—which he gets at the second-hand clothing store. Therefore, what is too big on one hero is too tight on someone else. The good novelist doesn't know how to paint *backgrounds,* but circumstances, outlines. In the good novel, the trees, the mountains, and the clouds, are so many other living beings involved in the plot. Whatever is distant from the live character is useless in the novel. It may do for the theater: at least for poor theater."[34] Jarnés is interested in personifying inanimate objects, as well as depersonalizing people. The personalization of trees and mountains makes even more hypothetical the application of the term "dehumanized" to his novels. Even the trees are, in the author's view human. Essentially the "dehumanized" novel is involved with the re-ordering of reality. When Jarnés reifies people he is suggesting a new vision of reality. The human is present both as a viewer of this vision (Jarnés himself) and as a recipient of the vision (the reader).

Because of his avowed intent to fuse life and art, it is curious that the opinion persists that Jarnés and his generation produced a "dehumanized" art. It is quite common to find his generation dismissed as closed off, self-contained. José R. Marra-López be-lieves that "the mistake of that generation, perhaps in another regard the first Spanish effort of a group with a European dis-position, was not that it was *that way,* but that it was *that way in the novel,* instead of having chosen the essay or poetry."[35] His opinion is shared by Eugenio de Nora, who believes that "the very sense of those literary movements, dehumanizing, aseptic and antirealistic, was opposed, almost by definition, to any pos-sible maturity within the genre of the novel, condemning potential novelists to formalism and creative sterility."[36]

Jarnés in particular is singled out by critics as a notable failure in the novel. Gullón has written: "The best writers of the present day—Ayala or Cela, for example—have risen above the sense of inferiority felt by the Spanish novelists of a quarter of a century ago. Perhaps the excessive preoccupation with technique, or rather, techniques, from which that period suffered, limited too much the possibilities of talented writers such as Benjamín Jarnés and Antonio Espina."[37] Guillermo de Torre remarks: "And as for Jarnés . . . whom people remember today only to disparage him without having read him . . . Jarnés, as a novelist, paid too much tribute to his verbal gifts, his bedazzlement by Giraudoux; he was a victim of formalism and was excessively reticent, as were others of his period, toward the exterior world, the substance or germ of the novel."[38]

It seems that these objections are somewhat misplaced. Jarnés did not in fact propose a divorce between the novel and reality, but rather the transformation of the latter in the former. The antipathy, felt by critics seems due more to the poetic nature of Jarnés' novels. A willingness to allow Jarnés' vision of reality to permeate one's own is necessary for the appreciation of his novels, just as this is the prime necessity for the appreciation of poetry. In this sense, also, Jarnés is distinctly modern in that he insists on more participation, perhaps more effort to comprehend, from the reader than does a Realist novelist. It would seem unfair to fault Jarnés on this score while exalting other modern novelists, among them Faulkner, Unamuno, and Joyce who do the same thing.

Of course, the participation demanded by Jarnés of his reader is of a different sort than that demanded by Unamuno or Joyce. Jarnés' reader must enter the book to make coherent sense out of the characters' poetic perceptions, but not to complete a logical plot action, or to supply from evidence pieced together the basis for a character's motivations. Both types of participation have the aspect of problem solving, but the difference is one of magnitude.

When the reader supplies a missing link in a Joycean action, he is likely satisfying himself that he has accomplished something real. That is, when the reader discovers the specific place through which Bloom must have passed to reach, for example, Sandymount Beach, he feels that he has had a hand in the creation of a logical or real action. Often enough, in order to solve the riddles in a given novel, a reader must bring with him a knowledge of the geography of the novel's locale. In Jarnés' novels, the riddles to be solved center on a poetic link or an analogy which is missing from the page but which exists in the character's mind with sufficient force to propel him to the next action or perception.

But finding the missing links in a poetic analogy, completing a poetic perception, does not have the same sense of reality about it for the usual reader that a map of Dublin has. Hence, the reader gains an understanding of the character as the author has wished him to have it, but not anything of a nature external to the character. This is, at once, Jarnés' aim and the reason why his critics call his works hermetic.

Some critics charge the assumed failures of this generation's novels to Ortega. Surely, when Ortega asserted, for example, that the possible themes in the novel had been exhausted and that the theme of a novel was not what interested the reader—but that its treatment was—he was overlooking the fact that themes in the novel, or in any literary form for that matter, have almost always been used up. That is, the supposed exhaustion of novelistic themes was not peculiar to the 1920's, and therefore was an insufficient cause or explanation of the genre's demise. In Spain's Golden Age, the surfeit of honor plays demonstrates that trite themes were no obstacle either to the production or enthusiastic reception of *comed'as*. In a still earlier age, the chivalric novels were noted as much for their trite themes as for their handling of these themes; yet they too enjoyed an enormous vogue. In fact, we could say that within a given genre, the themes are always limited, but that this does not of itself bring about the extinction of the genre.

What changes and develops is the relationship between the author and the themes, not merely the style of the author. The difference between Galdós and Baroja, for example, is not mainly stylistic. Their subject matter (theme) is substantially the same. And though Galdós was panoramic in his coverage of Madrid society, he did not exhaust its themes or the Realist novel as a genre. Baroja comes to the same subject matter and writes novels which are not great innovations in the stylistic sense with respect to Galdós'. Baroja's uniqueness consists essentially in that he goes beyond Galdós in his rejections and condemnations.

In addition to being held responsible for the supposed infertility of Jarnés' generation in the novel, Ortega has been challenged in his capacity as a critic. He had written, in 1914, that "reading poetry is not one of my usual occupations."[39] Chabás, seeking to discredit Ortega's position as a critic, wrote: "The discerning reader will perhaps not forget when considering the theory of the novel of Ortega y Gasset, that he himself has declared: "I acknowledge that I am a very poor reader of novels.' This confession explains how he could have testified as to the crisis of a genre when there were still alive and at at the height of their production in Spanish, Baroja, Unamuno, Gallegos, Eustaquio [*sic*] Rivera, Mariano Azuela, etc. . . ."[40] One cannot dispense with Ortega's theory merely by quoting remarks which were made out of a sense of humility, real or feigned. Substantial work would be required to disprove Ortega's capacities as a critic or many of his critical insights. Where the philosopher wrote about so many aspects of the life and culture of his times, his anatogonist cannot discredit him merely by charging that he viewed literature from his own—and at the time almost unique in Spain—point of view.

Other facets of Ortega's relationship to his generation have been attacked. Max Aub says that Ortega's first mistake lay in thinking his ideas carried no weight; he believes that Ortega forgot that, "with the spread of culture, the Spaniard no longer hated the intellectual."[41] Aub further argues that the effect of Ortega's theorizing was to cut short any real talent there may have been in the novelists, by his pessimism and his insistence on the value and necessity of an anti-popular art (*ibid.*, p. 93). But these commentators are challenged by those who, like Emilia de Zuleta give due emphasis to the final words of Ortega's *Ideas on the Novel*. She points out that Ortega's comments were not the proclamation of a new creed, but merely the diagnosis of a novelistic fact of this period.[42]

In any case, it would seem that some misunderstanding of Ortega is at the root of the criticisms of the so-called "dehumanized novel." For in reality, Ortega's *The Dehumanization of Art* was essentially an essay on modern painting. And while it is possible to have a dehumanized painting, it is quite impossible to have a dehumanized novel.[43] This is due not only to the fundamental nature of the novel as an interpretation of human life; it is due also to the fact that the materials a novel must have on its surface are entirely different from those a painting must have.

A novel must offer human or at least humanoid figures. It must offer human language. If it does not, it must deal with abstractions. On the one hand, an abstract subject matter produces an essay; on the other, an abstract language produces a treatise in logic or mathematics. It is essential then to restrict the use of the term "dehumanized" to that particular trait of the Jarnesian novel which mechanizes the human being. For in all other regards, Jarnés' novels are profoundly human. Their attempt to renovate the conventional view of reality, their attempt to present a childlike view of the world—these are efforts which are filled with both a human presence (the novelist) and a human product (poetry).

All the objections to the poetry in Jarnés' novels, to his supposed misapplication of Orteguian theory, seem to respond to a fundamental dissatisfaction which readers encounter when they approach the Jarnesian novel. This dissatisfaction has many roots. First of all is the objection that Jarnés' language is frivolous or factitious. His style is commonly attacked for its "acrobatics."[44] There is some truth in this charge, for Jarnés proposed strict adherence not to logical thinking, nor to the ordered rhetorical expression of "academic" verse, but to the expression of the fresh vision of the child before the world.

In attempting to view the world through a child's eyes, Jarnés presents what seems precariously like an autistic and hermetic novel, and he appears to be regressing symbolically. And since the child's thinking seems sometimes frivolous, so may Jarnés' language. Remarking on this tendency in artists, Kenneth Burke has written: "Symbolic regression becomes dangerous insofar as the artist permits his medium to depart too far from the forensic texture (otherwise stated: insofar as he overstresses 'self-expression' and understresses 'communication'). . . . But, fortunately, the destruction of a forensic texture is always far from absolute— the difference between stable and unstable forensic textures is merely relative—hence, there is no need, other than the author's private ambitions, for a complete regression to autistic thought."[45] Jarnés' symbolic regression, his cultivating a child's point of view, is only relative. Surely his language seems at times hermetic, because of its high degree of stylization. And although it may reduce the possibilities of communicating to a large audience, its departure from conventional language is not so great as to have prevented the small group which Jarnés considered his primary audience from understanding and appreciating his works.

The attacks of critics like Nora embody a bias against what we might today call the uncommitted writer. To some extent a similar bias can also be seen in Camus' remarks on an author who was one of Jarnés' favorites. Camus commented that

Giraudoux's art consisted solely of "replacing the great themes of fatality by acrobatics performed by the intelligence."[46]

Furthermore, the reader's demand that the novel be lifelike, *verosímil,* is not met. Any published novel exists in a social context. Aside from the fact that it is produced for an audience, and that the author receives money for having produced it, the novel's social situation involves its role as an agent of the communicative process between author and reader. The demand for lifelikeness which the reader makes is based on his need to rely, to some extent, on a conventional portraiture in the novel. Without the conventionality the communicative process is made more difficult, because there is no longer a commonly accepted language, no longer an accepted convention of communication.

The attempt at the poetic novel was, as Rosa Chacel has pointed out, a beginning, a first step toward the formulation of a new convention; but she adds that "the profusion of novels arising in Spain lately does not begin here, it does not tell us about the post-Orteguian Spaniard. That Spaniard and that Spain burst like a bubble, and the most curious thing is that the onlookers watched it with as much naturalness as if it were really a soap bubble."[47] This poignant comment indicates the rebuff which the reading public and later novelists alike administered to Jarnés' generation.

One reason advanced to explain this rebuff is that the aesthetics of the novel have changed. The present-day reader is thought to be reluctant to accept "art for art's sake," psychological or stylistic narcissism, moral vagueness or irresponsibility. This is dubious for two reasons. First, there is not, nor has there ever been, an aesthetic canon for the novel.[48] Although we can formulate rules *a posteriori* which can account for most of what happens in a specific sort of novel, these rules are always descriptive, never prescriptive. The writer who followed such rules and tried to write another *Don Quixote* would not duplicate Cervantes' novel. If he were gifted he might succeed in writing a novel as great; but the essential ingredient would be his talent. Secondly, the popularity and critical esteem achieved by novelists like Robbe-Grillet, Beckett, Cela, Cortázar, and Barth, to name only a few, show that some of the principal traits of the Jarnesian novel so severely stigmatized by critics are applauded by and effective with the modern reader.

In much of the critical literature on this period one finds the assumed failure of the Jarnesian novel charged to its anti-popular character.[49] Clearly both Ortega's and Jarnés' theoretical positions on the novel can justify their being called anti-popular. But this explains nothing except the failure of Jarnés novels to gain wide readership. It does not explain why the inherent artistic merits of Jarnés' position failed to be exploited by other writers who followed him closely in time.

The cause is probably historical. Ayala, explaining his own apostasy from the aesthetics of "dehumanization" at the end of the 1920's, says that in view of the grave events which loomed on the political horizon in Europe "that literary toying, aestheticist and gratuitous, to which we were devoted" had no meaning.[50] Particularly from the beginning of the Second Republic in 1931, the politicization of culture which had been going on in Spain since the turn of the century was intensified. Works of art were increasingly being judged by intellectuals according to how well they expressed an awareness of the problems which had been identified and marked for early action by the social and political programs of the Republic. This is not to say that literary and artistic judgments had never been rendered from political grounds before. But now there was a pervasive sense among a great many intellectuals of the need to solve pressing problems; the reforms of the Republic (e.g., secularization of the schools, the divorce law, Basque and Catalan separatism) seemed destined to modernize Spain fundamentally. A similar politicization was occurring in Europe and America, sometimes with the impetus of writers who advanced a doctrinaire Marxism, sometimes merely aided by those who were moderate Leftists, Socialists and liberals.[51]

In Spain, the Generation of 1927 had set about renovating literature according to the aesthetics of dehumanization. Ortega's *Revista de Occidente* had published Dámaso Alonso's groundbreaking rehabilitation of Góngora, and had reviewed Gerardo Diego's anthology of modern Gongorist verse. The impulse to style held sway in poetry and prose, and the attention of the writer was directed mostly to style rather than to subject matter. Hence, he could be said to be ignoring social problems. But such a single-mindedness is, after all, what provides a basis for homogeneity in a group of writers; it is the basis for artistic schools. There was reason to believe that the Generation's canon would have become more elastic and wide-ranging in its acceptance of the social milieu. Ayala had already forsaken his early aestheticism. A year before the outbreak of the Civil War, Antonio Espina was predicting a hopeful new stage of development for the Generation.[52] In fact, barely a month before the war started, Lorca had said: "No real man believes any more in that trifling pure art, art for art itself. At this dramatic moment in the world, the artist must laugh and cry with his people . . ."[53]

The change of direction would certainly have reduced the antipopular quality of the Generation's work. Sender, for one, although not a member of the Jarnés-Ortega circle, was already showing the way.[54] And if the novelists of the Generation had not produced significant novels,[55] it was merely a question of time until they did.[56] The striking and alarming implications in the word "dehumanization" were perhaps unfortunate because they prevented many from realizing that Ortega's formulations were but an elaboration of his view of art as stylization.[57] The misunderstanding of Ortega's and Jarnés' aesthetics of the novel obscured the fact that it was essentially an aesthetic in the humanistic tradition.[58] It still vouchsafed a position of primacy to the artist; and if it called for a reduction to the minimum of recognizable human characters, it did not demand their elimination. Later developments, mainly the "new wave" novels of Robbe-Grillet, come much closer to what people thought Ortega meant by "dehumanization."

Thus, while hope for the future of the Generation's novel was being expressed, and many fertile possibilities for the novel lay in the future, the Civil War overtook the Generation of 1927. The war dispersed the most prominent members of the group, scattering them into exile, truncating the continuity of place and personality so necessary to the existence of a literary generation. The war and its aftermath effectively precluded any continuing native Spanish development in the trends espoused by the Generation.[59] Only in the 1950's was it possible to see in the Spanish novel some of the developments which might have arisen out of the Jarnesian novel.

In actuality, Spanish novelists of the '50's come to espouse certain principles akin to Jarnés' not through having read and been influenced by his novels, but rather through their assimilation of the works of non-Spanish authors, mainly the French, English, and Americans. Nonetheless, in Goytisolo, the late Luis Martín Santos, the Cela of *Mrs. Caldwell habla con su hijo,* we can see a concern with verbal artistry and novelistic structure which, without obliterating the social milieu, gives an emphasis to style which is directly in line with the aesthetic of Jarnés.

CHAPTER 3

The Novels

I El profesor inútil (The Useless Professor)

THREE years after Ortega y Gasset founded the *Revista de Occidente* in 1923, the publishing house of the same name began issuing a series of works, mostly prose, by younger writers. *El profesor inútil (The Useless Professor)* was the second of this series.[1] It was widely reviewed and on the whole well received. Perhaps because it was Jarnés' first novel—the *Mosén Pedro (Father Pedro)* of 1924 being a biography—it has been taken as typical of the rest of the author's novelistic production.[2] There is some validity for such an assumption since *The Useless Professor* shows a concern for generic problems which can also be seen in Jarnés' later work.

In its first edition, the book consisted of four loosely related episodes dealing with a Don Juan type whose major avocation is to follow girls in the streets. The third episode was "The Faithful River" which, as we mentioned previously (see p. 17 above) had come to Ortega's attention and had been published in the *Revista de Occidente* in 1925. In the second edition, the original was made approximately half again as long by the addition of a fifth tale, a prologue and an epilogue.[3] One recurrent practice Jarnés followed is his amplifying and lengthening his novels by including in them stories, essays, and dialogues which he had written earlier but had not published. Also, when his books went into a second or subsequent edition, they were often enlarged by the addition of material borrowed from other works of the author.

The concern for generic problems, for the definition of the novelistic genre, was an outgrowth of the crisis which was felt to exist in the genre in the 1920's. One implication of the Jarnesian practice of altering the book's contents, including in it prose matter composed for other books or on other occasions, is that the Jarnesian novel was not a fixed or unchangeable entity. Its contours could be altered at will to accommodate new material. Since there is no "plot line" in the traditional sense, new episodes grafted onto an existing novel do not disrupt the book's internal coherence. They do not serve, as in a serialized novel, to prolong the fictional trajectories of the characters; but neither do they support entirely the description of Jarnés' novels as thoroughly hermetic. For if a short story can be included in a novel, and if the novel can swell in a second edition by an injection of new fictional matter, then we are not dealing with a self-contained, impermeable world. Because of this fact, the novel might also be accused of being badly finished off, not well rounded, artistically incomplete. On the other hand, it could be said in the author's defense that such a novel was closer to real life, more of a living thing itself, and like a living being, adaptable and capable of growth.

We called the four episodes "loosely related" because their only unifying thread is the sensibility and continuity of the protagonist, the useless professor. The first tale relates his employment as the tutor of Valentín and his attraction to Valentín's sister, Ruth. He resists her flirtations, more out of timidity than rectitude, until she frankly offers to give him a lesson in love. His acceptance of the offer and the ensuing seduction are veiled by "silence and shadow" (p. 98).

The second episode tells of the professor's meeting a girl in the park who tells him that she had lived in Paris and had an unhappy love affair. She is now a governess in the employ of a diplomat. When they part, he goes to an exhibition of poster art, and sees on one of the posters a nude pose of the governess. Turning around, he finds her behind him, and they go off together. He will enjoy her living beauty while the gallery-goers will only enjoy the lifeless rendering of the poster.

In the third episode, "The Faithful River," the professor and his student, Carlota, find each other more interesting than the lessons at hand. In consequence, she fails her examinations. They meet on a bridge over the Ebro and she writes his name on her report card and throws it into the river. He says that the failing grade will outlive his name, since the latter was written in pencil on the card.

In the final story, "Trótula," the action is divided into two parts. In the first the protagonist meets Rebeca, who is carrying a pitcherful of curative waters from Trótula, a *curandera,* to her mother who is gravely ill. He persuades her to tarry with him one afternoon, and later, to hasten Rebeca's arrival home, he fills the pitcher with ordinary water. The girl's mother drinks this and dies. In the second part of the story, the protagonist goes to see the *curandera* and learns that she is going to avenge his substitution of the water by sticking pins into a picture of him which Rebeca had given her. He becomes more interested in witchcraft, but when he discovers that Trótula is in reality an appealing young woman, he decides that her magic is a sham. He goes to the park and throws Rebeca's picture into a pool. The next day he learns that she drowned while swimming with friends.

None of these episodes is either innovative in theme or original in treatment. They hang together through the glimpses each one sheds on the actions and personality of the protagonist. The prose throughout is concise and spare, with very few lengthy sentences, and a goodly amount of dialogue. Since the story line in each tale is so minimal, the bulk of the prose is devoted to descriptions of the protagonist's perceptions of the world around him, especially of the beauty of the female characters. Since we will examine the artistic qualities of the prose below in Chapter 4, we shall limit ourselves here to a presentation of some of the themes which appear in *The Useless Professor* and which signal major lines of development for our author's later work.

One of these themes is that of myth. In the prologue to *The Useless Professor,* Jarnés says that as a youth he felt himself surrounded by myths and came to consider himself a creator of myths (p. 8). "Myth is a little bit of humanity which has passed through the heavens. Without human fever, there could never have been mythology. Without mythology, human life would hardly have been more than a little sap, humors which come and go" (p. 18). Man is surrounded by "Antigone and Oedipus, Narcissus and Juno. Sylphs, gnomes, and ondines besiege us . . . The earth is a deficient copy of heaven. On it—and on the sea and in the air—the gods and demigods, fallen heroes, myths once improved on, come and go in disguise" (p. 30).

In this novel the theme of myth is present in the "Trótula" episode for, being a *curandera* whose magic actually works, she

is made to reenact her traditional mythical role.[4] While Jarnés
was seldom to devote himself to the rewriting or modernization
of ancient myths in their entirety, his fondness for them reappears frequently, e.g., in *Viviana y Merlín (Vivien and Merlin)*,
1930, and in the recurrent presence of Walkyries, elves and
other mythical beings.

The twentieth century has seen a new vogue for myths in many
areas of culture. The findings of archaeology and anthropology,
the conceptual framework of Freudian and Jungian psychology,
the fictional exploitation of myth by writers such as Giraudoux,
Gide, G. B. Shaw, Sartre, all point to the prominence of myths.
For Jarnés, the reliance on myth provides a structure or frame
for the perception and acceptance of the phenomenal world. That
the reliance is neither constant nor overemphasized shows that
the author's demand for structure was not all-embracing. That is,
while the use of myth is often to be found in Jarnés, it is never
as a rigid system controlling an entire work throughout that we
find it. It recurs and disappears, casually, at points where Jarnés
wishes to invoke some authority for his own perception. Thus, to
bolster his assertion of Trótula's evil intentions, he invokes
Lucifer whom he calls "the Father of History" (p. 172). Or, to
shed more light on Ruth, he calls her "Disorder" (p. 109).

The use of myth in this way relieves the author of the necessity
of either telling or showing us (through dramatic situation) any
of the traits ascribed to the characters. Where the Realist would
depict one in problematic conflict with an idea, Jarnés often as-
signs characters their traits through myth. This presupposes in
the reader a knowledge of the myth, and is one trait which leads
Jarnesian critics and commentators to speak of his anti-popular-
ism. It also makes up one large element of Jarnés' prose which
may discourage some readers: its allusiveness. For if a characteristic, such as disorderliness, is ascribed to Ruth casually, without
the presentation of situations which evidence the disorder, the
reader may feel deprived of the chance to get to know Ruth
fully. He may feel that the allusion to her disorderliness is insufficient for him to accept her as a character. However, in this
work, Jarnés is not concerned with the delineation of characters
so much as with the way they appear to the eyes of the useless
professor, a spectator who seldom acts, whose shyness is almost
paralyzing.

Still another effect of the use of myth is that it places the character who is treated mythically, or endowed with traits which come from myths, into a pattern of present-time reality, of instantaneousness, much as a photograph would do. That is, if Trótula is evil because she embodies a mythical influence from Lucifer, then questions relating to Trótula's past experience, her development as a character, "how she got that way," are thoroughly idle. For if myths are all about us in the air, then any character singled out by the author may be a sort of precipitate of mythical influences. He is functioning more as a "real" manifestation of those intangible influences than as a personality which is the result of a development through imagined experiences of his own in the novel and through the influence of other characters in the work. What this does is to short-circuit the usual attempts the reader may make at explaining the conduct of the characters, or at understanding their actions as specific points of an extended fictional trajectory. Thus none of the characters, not even the professor himself, is an imagined being one juncture of whose existence is visible because the author has revealed it to us. Rather, all the characters are fixed, invariate, acting only in response to their natures at the moment. If part of their natures embodies a myth, then it too is as active in leading to the specific behavior they carry out as is another part, let us say, the timidity of the professor.

It is in this particular view of character that we find Jarnés reacting to two special circumstances of his life. The first was the unhappiness and difficulties of his own childhood and young manhood. The second was the influence of Surrealism and Freudianism. Jarnés was aware of Freud's teachings about early childhood experience; in the prologue to this work he says: "The destiny of the adult is already predetermined in the psychic experiences of infancy" (p. 23). Elsewhere he had written, borrowing an epigraph from Kierkegaard: "My whole existence has been a struggle against myself."[5] In that same preface, he remarked that he did not want to face again all his past "egos" which, despite their indecisiveness and haziness, ought to be respected and sympathized with. Whether because of the painful memories of his childhood and his false starts on other careers, or because of embarrassment or fear of what his early experience might reveal about his adult life, Jarnés rejected the Freudian view of personality. He recognized some of its potential validity but refused to apply it to his fictional characters or to himself. His readers are invited to such application, however, because Jarnés readily admitted that his characters were incarnations of himself.[6]

Jarnés' antipathy to Surrealism is based partly on his resistance to the precepts of Freudian psychology. The useless professor says: "I feel someone pushing me from step to step toward the cellars of the unconscious, and I'm afraid of being turned into the hero of a Surrealist novel" (p. 74). And in 1927, Jarnés wrote: "Surrealism is always active in the cellar, and its emblem is the Freudian crab."[7] It has long been common for Freudian psychology to be stigmatized for its "underground" nature; the mysterious and hidden or forgotten influences of the past which motivate present conduct can be attacked for their malevolence, irrationality, and inaccessibility to reason. Likewise, Jarnés disavows Surrealism because of its dependence upon the unconscious sources of artistic material.[8]

While Jarnés rejects a Freudian position and Surrealism as elements in his artistic production, he is willing to grant to myth an almost equivalent motivating power. The difference is that he does not go beneath the surface of the myth to seek explanations in line with modern abnormal psychology.

Another implication in the avoidance of Freudian or other depth psychology is that the view of character as frozen in the present moment like a photograph, is reinforced. For indeed, if we may not inquire into the imagined histories of the characters to seek explanations of their natures, then the characters are deprived of any history at all. They are not vital, changing creatures; influenced by their past *and* present, and capable of having an imaginable future existence once the book is ended. They are merely present before us now, bereft of past or future. Of course, one source of the derision meted out to the Realist novelist is his propensity to explain, in an epilogue, the destinies of his characters which lie outside the compass of the narrative.

Thus, Jarnés' characters by and large have no vital trajectories. They do not rise from obscurity, surmount difficulties, and decline into respected old age. Nor do they assume in their course of action in a given novel any mythical stature except a momentary one. Their mythical qualities are taken on and put aside when a particular situation demands. This makes the depiction of a given character a set of distinct portraits which are unified only by being of the same character. Each momentary portrait is self-sufficient, fragmentary, and discrete. We can see how such a handling of character facilitates the addition of new fictional material when the novel goes into a second edition. The characters, as well as the story line itself, are open-ended for they have neither beginning nor end.

This open-endedness endows Jarnés' characters with a certain freedom. They are not bound by the limitations of their past or their social class. They are not the inevitable result of the working out of definable social laws, nor are they a consequence of the sinister and subterranean manipulations of their unconscious. Rather, they are very nearly "blithe spirits," Ariels, who thrive in the open air, come and go at the author's whim. The freedom and openness inherent in his characters allow Jarnés free rein for the employment of his perception of the poetry in everyday life.

In one respect, however, the useless professor is limited. Along with his propensities for following women, he displays a timidity which is almost impossible for him to break out of. Referring to Ruth, he says: "Woman comes out to meet love when love is shy" (p. 67). And it is largely upon the tacit or expressed invitations of the women in his life that the professor enters into an affair with them. Thus, he is not a Don Juan conquering women by the force of his masculinity; he fortunately finds acquiescence where Don Juan at times found resistance.

The professor's timidity is an aspect of a generalized passivity which befits his role as a spectator of life. His function is to take in the experiences life affords him, and transform them into poetry in the telling. It would be out of character for him to seek experiences of his own accord, that is, for him to have ambitions for his life. Thus, in his relations with Ruth's brother, Valentín, he is put to considerable trouble and a long peregrination across Madrid—in an episode which recalls Galdós' Máximo Manso and Manolo Peña in *El amigo Manso*—because he accedes to Valentín's wish that he accompany him. It is true he had a vague hope of meeting Ruth (p. 73), but its vagueness keeps it from being as strong a motivation as Valentín's insistence.

We see the same passivity at another point in the book. When

Luisa fails to keep her date with the professor at a café, he says he was just as happy: "Free and alone, wasn't I at the doorway of a new adventure?" (p. 180). Rather than anger or a resolve to pursue her, Luisa's not appearing gives rise to an even-tempered acceptance of whatever new adventures may arise. The professor does not seek out the new adventure; he waits for it to present itself. Likewise, Jarnés wrote that in order to reach immortality it was necessary not to interfere with events; one should "let himself be carried docilely toward the epilogue which the gods are to set out" (p. 252).

The passivity of the professor implies acceptance of what events and life bring him. Also, the passive protagonist is an anti-hero in embryo, for in him we find several anti-heroic traits: refusal to act, aimlessness, exposure to the whim of fate. The professor conveys no feeling that Jarnés has worked out the implications of his passivity, or that it represents a coherent philosophical viewpoint. Rather it is merely a fact of the professor's character, which might almost as well have been the reverse.

As the professor watches some children making paper boats out of newspapers, and floating them in a pool in the park, he muses: "What a pleasure to destroy a whole past that way. . . . What a terrific joke it would be on the gloomy Old Man, if I sank all my past years into the water, and came out at the side of the pool turned into another child, with only one will, that of being committed to the events of the moment" (p. 237). Aside from an echo of myths of symbolic rebirth in water—as surveyed by Otto Rank in his *The Myth of the Birth of the Hero*—we notice in this passage a willingness to give up the personality one has become in order to assume a new one, the personality of a child.

When one holds that personality does not develop, but merely *is*, then it is easy to wish that one could be reborn as another. One can ignore the obvious possibility that the child one is reborn as will be heir to similar or equally unfortunate experiences as oneself. Of course, the wish and willingness to be reborn depends in part on some underestimation of what one is at the moment, and upon a dubious view of what one, if he is not reborn, might become in the future. However, the dramatic emphasis, as is true of the fictional character of the professor as a whole, is on the present, the rebirth, the action taken "now" which changes or improves one's lot. The importance of the past and of the future, in consequence, suffers a considerable reduction.

Taking a wider view of this question, it should not seem odd that Jarnés places primary emphasis on the present. He had achieved success as a writer published by prestigious reviews only after a lengthy and presumably unhappy series of experiences, first in his family, and then in the seminary and in the Army. Those beginning their literary careers with him in the mid-1920's were similarly impressed by the fertility of the new artistic movements. Jarnés was moved, as they were, to explore the vein of the poetic novel as fully as possible. He was not concerned with long-range plans for the construction of a body of work; rather he was interested in making each single work he published as perfect as he could. We can safely assume that it would have taken some years for the influence of Jarnés' prose to be felt among the Spanish novelists, and for his contribution to be incorporated into the ongoing Spanish novelistic tradition. Perhaps now, after a twenty-year hiatus, we shall see his influence being made manifest.

II El convidado de papel (The Paper Guest)

The second of Jarnés' novels appeared in 1928.[9] It consists of a prologue and nine "notes," each of which treats an episode or facet of the experiences of Julio and Adolfo in the Seminary of Augusta. The autobiographical quality is apparent; many of Jarnés' novels are set in or refer to Zaragoza and the towns of Aragón.[10] The nine episodes are not related or unified by a plot line, except the slender one which recounts Julio's apparent submission to the seminary routine and his inner rebelliousness. The seminarians' life is described with detachment and irony, and a mild, bemused criticism is levelled at the priests' foibles, their wrong-headed morality, their attempts to mold all the students into a single conforming type.

This novel has a certain unity of character lacking in *The Useless Professor*. Where in the latter book the professor seems adaptable to the demands of each new prospective conquest in each of the episodes, Julio has fundamentally a more unchanging role. To a much lesser extent than the professor, Julio shifts his affections, turning from one conquest to the next without regret and with relish for the new adventure. In *The Paper Guest*, unity is afforded also by the fact that the setting, the seminary and the city of Zaragoza, is unchanged, and that there are several secondary characters who remain visible throughout.

There is no concern for chronology in *The Paper Guest;* each of the episodes occurs independently and they could all be shuffled in order without doing any great violence to the book's coherence. They are, thus, separate pieces of a mosaic whose major attraction is one of tone and color. As was the case in *The Useless Professor,* one or another episode could be subtracted, or new ones added, without substantially changing this picture of seminary life.

In taking up the theme of seminary life, Jarnés was to become a member of a rather large group of Spanish novelists who have written on the same theme. Some of the more prominent of them are: Juan Valera, *Pepita Jiménez* (1874); Pérez de Ayala, *A.M.D.G.* (1910); Arturo Barea, *La forja* (the first volume of his trilogy, *La forja de un rebelde* [1946]); and Ramón Sender, *Hipógrifo violento* (1954). In regard to Valera, Jarnés renders a conclusive opinion in *The Paper Guest.* He dismisses Valera as fundamentally a Romantic, and his priest hero as hopelessly middle-class. Where Pérez de Ayala delivers a stinging denunciation of the Jesuit seminary in *A.M.D.G.,* Jarnés focusses more upon Julio's self-possessed introspection in the face of the difficulties of the school routine. Where folly or cruelty serves Pérez de Ayala as a basis for bitter criticism, they serve Jarnés as a motive for one of Julio's flights of fantasy. *The Paper Guest* portrays some of the rigidities of seminary life as well as the privations the students are subjected to; but unlike Barea and Sender, whose novels do the same, Jarnés is not socially oriented. He is not really concerned with the social organization of the school, its mirroring of social flaws in Spain generally. He wants primarily to portray Julio's spiritual and artistic individuality and the way in which his flights into fantasy provide an escape valve for his amorous emotions and his sensitivity. Thus, for example, during matins, Julio imagines the "peculiar secret vices" of the Scriptural characters (p. 88).

There are two types of "paper guest" in the novel. One type consists of the photographs and love letters received secretly by Adolfo and Julio from their girl friends, Eulalia and Estrella. The other "paper quest" is a copy of Stendhal's *Le Rouge et le noir*

which, passed from hand to hand clandestinely, provides Julio
with his first acquaintance with his namesake, Julien Sorel, whom
he comes to admire enthusiastically. One of these paper guests, a
love letter from Eulalia, is discovered in Adolfo's room during
a surprise inspection, and brings about his expulsion from the
seminary. Adolfo had decided to leave anyway; when Julio
finds him gone, he leaves the seminary and rushes to Estrella.
There he embraces her joyfully and, looking about the room,
discovers "Adolfo, sweetly submerged in the harsh clarity of
his paper guest made flesh" (p. 233). In a mocking pun upon
Tirso's *Burlador de Sevilla y convidado de piedra,* Jarnés is suggesting that the pursuit of women and of the flesh leads not to
perdition but to salvation. For if both Adolfo's and Julio's
thoughts are occupied, in the absence of any feelings of clerical
vocation, in the conjuring of feminine beauty, their embrace of
Eulalia and Estrella and their leaving the seminary is a move
toward greater concreteness and satisfaction in their lives.

Julio's devotion to women is a devotion to an abstraction. If he
can change, as he does, the object of his fantasies from Nieves, to
Luscinda, to Estrella, then there is no reason to think that Estrella
holds any special place in his affections. Although the novel ends
with their embrace, nothing in their relations justifies a belief that
Julio has become monogamous all at once. Were the reader to
imagine a prolongation to this novelistic action he could logically
conclude that Julio might one day tear up Estrella's photograph
and throw it into the Ebro, as he had once done with Nieves'.
Estrella is desired not for any unique qualities she possesses as
Estrella but because she is a living example of womanhood and
as such, not only a necessary corrective to the celibacy and
hysterical misogyny of the seminary, but an ingredient essential
to Julio's leading a full life. In Ortega's words, placed as an
epigraph to this novel: "How can we reach a full life without
woman, without the cultivator of the feelings?" Estrella fills a
void in Julio's life; she brings him the life of the sentiments
which was denied him in the seminary. And with her sentiments
she brings the joys of the flesh.

But, again all this is being worked out on an abstract, almost
essayistic, plane. Their relationship in all its fullness serves as the
climax to, rather than the substance of, this novel. Estrella, for all
the considerable demands of her role as partner to the sensitive

and lustful Julio, remains on the whole a shadow of a character. Like almost all the secondary characters in Jarnés' novels, she is depicted with broad strokes, no attention being given to her motivations. Jarnés seems to acknowledge this when he has Estrella ask if she will always be just a paper guest (p. 89), i.e., whether she will be allowed to enter his life only as an epistolary lover, akin to the characters in the books which were smuggled into the seminary. But even when Julio leaves the seminary, there is little indication that Estrella will hold any but a temporary reality for him.

This is not to say that their relationship, because it is impermanent, has no impact on the reader. If it were permanent it would tend toward matrimony which is strongly attacked as a bourgeois institution in the pointed comments Julio exchanges with Adolfo on the subject of the four couples who inhabit four apartments visible from the balcony of the seminary. Its impermanence does not affect its pivotal role in freeing Julio from the seminary. In this way, it makes its impact on the reader as the thing which, at the end of Julio's long experience in the seminary, points to a new possibility for his life.

The impact of their relationship, further, is not in that it frees Julio from any sexual inhibition, of which he had by that time little enough. It merely releases him from the claims of his clerical career for which he had had no particular vocation. Perhaps because of this, Estrella need not embody great uniqueness and attraction; the seminary's claims on Julio's allegiance were already quite weak.

The prologue tells us a little about Julio's childhood and his discovery of himself. As a child, Julio used to skip on his way to school. Metaphorizing and enlarging upon this very common and trivial occurrence, Jarnés tells us that "his feet learned a voluptuous new theory of contacts [with the stones of the road]" (p. 10). Seeing large theoretical implications in the simple acts of simple people recalls Unamuno's Paparrigópulos (in *Amor y pedagogía*) who walked by geometry and digested by chemistry. What is new in Jarnés is the novelty of the theory: it is new for Julio because he is learning it for the first time. Also there is a reflection of the "new" sensibility in literature which belonged to Jarnés and his generation. The voluptuousness of the tactile is a prominent theme in Jarnés. And added to all this is

Jarnés' view of the child as a being specially endowed for the experience of art, because his youth connotes innocence.

In Julio's case, his innocence is quickly breached by the beautiful school teacher who comes to town. She is Eulalia who, in later incarnations in the novel, is to be the mistress first of Adolfo's uncle and then of Adolfo (p. 177). In the prologue Eulalia is allowed to impersonate a mythical character; every morning during her sunbath she changes into a submissive Danaë (p. 31). She is so fond of Julio that she offers to buy him a pair of shoes; but he prefers to go barefooted for the voluptuous pleasures it gives him. As their intimacy progresses, Julio caresses Eulalia's breast and discovers with astonishment "that a marvelous power flows from his hands: that of making matter vibrate, that of eliciting its sweetest sounds" (p. 32). In an image that echoes Pygmalion, as well as the Russian proverb about woman being like a balalaika, Jarnés injects an additional element, albeit covertly: Julio becomes momentarily Zeus. For if Eulalia is Danaë, then her lover, Julio, is Zeus. Jarnés does not elaborate on the mythical role Julio enacts, but that role is the symbolic link between Julio's early and manly ability to make Eulalia tremble with a caress, and his dawning awareness of himself as an artist. That is, the amorous and artistic abilities are raised to the same level of divinity: "And he looks at his hands, astonished, these tender hands of a child, marvelous instrument by means of which the eternal impulses of art and love are awakened in stone and flesh" (p. 33).

When Julio proclaims, in lines which parallel those which end *A Portrait of the Artist as a Young Man:* "I shall forge the first links in a long chain of dialogues; I shall weave a metaphorical frieze" (p. 49), his growing self-awareness reaches proportions similar to those of Stephen Dedalus.[11] We can see the clear-cut identity Jarnés establishes between the creativity of art and love. For the author, as for a great many of his novelistic characters, to be an artist is to be a lover, a lover of objects, of women, of sensations, of all of life.

Like so many other instances in Jarnés' work, however, this ascension of Julio's to a sort of cosmic creativity is merely stated, not developed fictionally. As if the author feared falling into a Romantic frenzy, he breaks off Julio's rise at its inception. For the episodes which follow this prologue do not show a character who is endowed with godlike artistic sensibilities and capacities; Julio's visions of the world make up a poetry in praise of the homely. The reader finds no Apollonian view, but rather a ground-level perspective, ever shifting and therefore varied, but lacking any real sense of urgency, either personal or social. In following Ortega's example and cultivating a perspectivist approach,[12] Jarnés avoids the fixed vantage point of the character who, even while meeting new experiences through the novel, retains a single and singular identity. By undercutting suggestions of Julio's divinity, he manages to keep him firmly rooted in the commonplace life around him.

Whatever Jarnés' private ambitions for his own career in the renovation of literary values, he does not allow Julio or his useless professor to swell to superhuman proportions. Thus there is no apocalyptic tone in the Jarnesian hero such as we find in Stephen Dedalus. Where Unamuno's claim that he was the *homo hispanicus* was a patent of typicality with which he justified his prescriptions for Spaniards as a race, Jarnés' heroes limit themselves to an acceptance of their typicality. Their creator undercuts them whenever they threaten to gain archetypal stature.

As the prologue ends, Julio prepares to enter the seminary. He prepares to become "a puppet of himself, who will never lose his mask of light-hearted ingenuousness" (p. 43). Such a pose gives him the self-protective coloration necessary to the retention of his integrity in the face of the various pressures of the school. For the first three days of the term, he keeps a diary, giving free rein in its pages to his fantasies. Unwittingly the seminary encourages such flights of fantasy. The obese priest, Mariano, does not object to the students' looking at the semi-nude women in magazines like *La Ilustración,* for he thinks it by far a worse sin to succumb to women in the flesh, "and he pardons easily any *delectatio morosa* with its fatal consequences" (p. 48). Jarnés, assiduous reader of Ortega's literary articles, follows his use of the same phrase in order to assert the equivalence between sins of action and sins of thought. For if fornication is a sin, imagination is no less a one. Again, art and love are brought into an equation; they are equally sinful in the eyes of the priest, therefore, equally desirable in Julio's.

Ultimately, however, cheesecake photographs and erotic novels are criticized, not for reasons of religious morality but because they are bad copies of real feminine beauty, and therefore lead the students to form illusions and false ideas (pp. 84-85). The imagination may serve as a sort of palliative therapy for the cloistered students. It may even have more directly beneficial effects. In the prologue, Eulalia's beauty was so arresting that all the men of the town used to imagine her while they were making love to their wives: "Eulalia worked the miracle of fertilizing sterile ground" (p. 27).

Julio's fantasy provides relief from a boring class as he imagines the teacher, *Monsieur,* jeered by a chorus of *olé's* and rising to his feet to receive a toast from the students who are holding "golden glasses of González Byas" (p. 105). Though such a scene may seem Surrealistic, it falls short of Surrealism because the author announces it as a fantasy. Thus, it is a waking dream, a metaphor which was thoroughly hypothetical. Jarnés' respect for the integrity of reality, its ineradicable realness, would tend to prevent his fusing fantasy with reality as a good Surrealist does. Also, as we saw above, Jarnés mistrusted Surrealism because of what he considered its dependence on sinister nether regions of the psyche. To allow Surrealistic irrationality to provide either method or matter for his novels would have been a violation of Jarnés' belief in the need for the artist to exercise conscious control over his art. Labelling the classroom fantasy as a fantasy allows him to introduce all the comic bite and hostile satire which Julio felt, and still retain conscious, indeed announced, control.

Though fantasy, just as the commonplace artifacts and events of everyday life, could provide the stimulus for fictional episodes, it had always to pass the editorial censor which was the author's artistic consciousness. In the exercise of his authorial control, Jarnés clearly and safely sets himself apart from those who, like the Dadaists and Surrealists, believed that almost anyone could write a poem or a novel by merely setting down, in glorious disarray, the material offered up by his unconscious. Jarnés frequently wrote of the novelist's task as an extension of the function of an editor or publisher. Near the end of *The Paper Guest,* Jarnés expressed the novelist's obligations in publishing terms: "It is everyone's inescapable duty to put out periodically, new and beautiful types of humanity, capable of slowly renewing the aesthetic face of the globe. If the warrior destroys whole editions, and the priest mutilates or blots out the text, the creator ought to follow behind them sowing the world with new, true 'copies' . . ." (pp. 219-20). Indeed, this statement at the outset of his career was to characterize accurately Jarnés' literary career in the long run.

Not only do his works offer a series of original and "true copies" of humanity, but they appear with the regularity and rhythmicity of an arm casting seed. We should notice that the creator *follows* the soldier and the priest, repairing the damage they wreak. He is not the embodiment or spokesman of his people; nor is he a trailblazer pointing out the necessary direction for others to follow. And while his hostility to the Army and the Church is obvious, and he is motivated to oppose their destructiveness, it is a hostility which never stoops to the use of its enemy's destructive weapons. Rather it is a resigned and almost congenial hostility which implacably but willingly opposes destruction with creation.

III   Paula y Paulita (Paula and Paulette)

Jarnés' third novel, *Paula y Paulita (Paula and Paulette),* appeared in 1929.[13] It is composed of two chapters bracketed by a *Nota preliminar* and a *Nota final*. The first chapter, "El número 479," is dated 1925-26; the second, "Petronio," is dated 1929. This book is another example of the ill-defined boundaries of the Jarnesian novel, for not only did Jarnés publish a short story under the same title in 1925,[14] but the novel's first chapter appeared under the title it bears in the novel in the Mexican review, *Ulises,* in December, 1927.

Like Jarnés' first two novels, indeed like almost all those he wrote, this novel has a negligible plot line. The first chapter relates the protagonist Julio's arrival at a spa called Balneario de Aguas Vivas, in actuality Alhama de Aragón, near Calatayud. The chapter title comes from the number of a room to which Julio is not assigned in the hotel. By mistake, he enters room 479 on the way to his own, surprising Paula, and beating an immediate if befuddled retreat. Paula, Paulita's mother, begins making plans to seduce Julio. He prefers her daughter, however, and successfully resists Paula's attentions until the very end of the chapter when he succumbs. Paulita is not interested in Julio because she is amorously involved with the spa's employee whose job it is to make the female guests fall in love with him.

At the end of the first chapter we meet the protagonist of the second, Mr. Brook, who was the business partner of Paula's deceased husband. In addition, he was Paula's lover and is the father of Paulita.[15] The second chapter, told from Brook's point of view in the third person, is largely a preparation for and justification of suicide. Its bulk consists of an account of a trip the foursome makes to a nearby monastery, the Abadía de los Fresnos, actually the Monasterio de Piedra, near Alhama. At the monastery, Brook discards his Baedecker and instead invents a series of fanciful and apocryphal histories relating to the features of the landscape and the monastery's past. In Brook's invented accounts appear several of the figures who become the subjects of later works by Jarnés: Viviana, the incarnation of the charm of feminine beauty and heroine of *Viviana y Merlín (Vivien and Merlin)*, and Eufrosina, the symbol of humor and grace and protagonist of *Eufrosina o la gracia (Euphrosyne or Grace)*.

Julio, a counterpart of the useless professor[16] and, we can be sure, a stand-in for Jarnés himself, seems essentially the observer of the action of this novel. His only initiatory acts involve the pursuit of Paulita; but he takes her rebuffs stoically and without rancor. In fact, in the first episode of the first chapter, when Julio mistakenly enters Paula's room, he does so out of an arithmetical mistake: he assumed that the rooms on his side of the corridor were all even-numbered, when in fact they were numbered consecutively. The mistake becomes the subject of dining-room gossip the next morning, when his waitress, not knowing Julio had been the intruder, relates the event to him. He discovers that he has become the hero of a gallant and romantic event retailed by the gossips. But contrary to the expectations of the other guests that he continue to act the part of the romantic hero of such a deed, he says: "I will never be the 'prime mover'—the old 'prime mover'—in any great or small chain of events" (p. 37).

Julio's passivity and renunciation of any chance to assert himself even extend to simple conversations. He remarks: "I can't tolerate an idea which doesn't go along with that of my companion. I don't believe in dialogue—a Platonic fable—and I always arrange my exterior monologue to accord with that of others"

(p. 56). These opinions of Julio's put him at the opposite pole from those in whom dialogue is the means, if not for an exchange of ideas with another and for an ensuing fertilization of thought, at least a means for self-assertion and an invitation to verbal confrontation. Julio, rather, submits to the ideas of his companions, preferring to observe them rather than assert his own. Behind this position we sense a certain feeling for decorum or courtesy which can be seen elsewhere in Jarnés' work. There is simply no sense of a struggle within Julio over the formation of either his ideas and opinions or of his personailty. Julio's continual reticence is designed to keep him from influencing the other characters.

How far we are with Julio from the Existentialist notions of "man making himself through action" or of "man making his personality through interaction with the other"! Julio's personality is fully formed, undergoes no changes, and in fact, hardly interacts with those of the other characters at all. Even when Paula seduces him at the end of the first chapter, he does not feel anything beyond self-effacement, the evasion of the limits of his personality; i.e., he loses himself in her.

In an important incident we see quite clearly the reasons why Julio stops short of any meaningful interaction with the other characters. One day, Paulita drops some apples she was carrying. Julio does not help her pick them up but merely watches as she does so. He tells us that Paulita "took my eagerness to taste brand-new [inéditas] beauty for serene unconcern" (p. 71). The brand-new beauty in question is the sight of Paulita's buttocks and hips as she bends over; they change from mere supports for her body into a voluptuous cupola to her youthful architecture. So, whatever impulse Julio might have felt to help her pick up the apples is short-circuited by the stronger urge to observe and record, on the artist's sensitive photographic plates, an original and beautiful perspective. We see here also a certain tendency to call beautiful whatever is new or original. No evidence apart from Julio's own opinion is offered by the author to confirm the fact that Paulita's position while bending over was beautiful. The fact that Julio had never seen her bend over that way before is enough to guarantee the beauty of her position.

To justify his refusal to help her, Julio tells Paulita about the feudal lord who used to make the prettiest girl in his town get undressed and then pick up some gold coins he'd scattered on the floor. Julio says the entire audience enjoyed the endless multiplication of beautiful profiles. When Paulita objects that such a thing was crude, Julio replies: "They were artists. Perhaps for the sake of a little blushing from the peasant girl, art would gain a brilliant canvas or a delightful sonnet" (p. 73). Although we are not prepared to call Julio's attitude inhuman—the situation after all is trivial—the lack of feeling in it does bespeak his total disinterest in meaningful interaction with others. For indeed, whatever beauty Julio perceives, and however artistically he later renders it in words for the reader, the fact is that the beautiful object, Paulita, derives no benefit from the episode, either in the way of recompense for having been made a little ridiculous, or in an increase in Julio's warm feelings for her. She is, in other words, merely the object of Julio's perception, not his partner in the creation of beauty.

It should also be noticed that Julio's relation with Paulita resembles another—Julio's relationship with Estrella (in *The Paper Guest;* see pp. 66-67 above). Both Julios use their women as means to an end, Estrella as the means of liberating Julio from his clerical career, Paulita as the means to the creation of brandnew types of beauty. Neither woman is desired for herself. It is not difficult to draw certain implications from such examples of egocentric love in Jarnés' heroes.

We would say, first of all, that the hero loves egocentrically because he considers himself essentially superior to, or more important than, the woman he loves. Such ideas of superiority which are not made particularly prominent in the heroes—since they are by-and-large non-heroic, retiring, and shy—do embody a basic narcissism which is common to Jarnés' heroes. They are narcissistic not only because of their absorption in their own perceptions of the world about them, and their self-imposed task of transmuting that world into poetry, but also because the novels themselves are hero-centered; i.e., in structural terms, they are narcissistically concerned with the inner worlds of the heroes, more than they are with the heroes' confrontations with others in their worlds. In the second place, egocentrism implies an undervaluation of the woman's ability to respond to the hero's love on other than a physical plane. This also may partially be determined by the structure of the Jarnesian novel; for if his heroines were depicted as spiritually and artistically the equals of his heroes, if they were not undervalued, then the focus of the novel would shift to a dual focus upon both characters. This would have the effect of robbing some of the hero's uniqueness as poetic artificer, and of reducing the intensity of the lyrical content of the hero's perceptions.

Further, since what is paramount is the creation of beauty, if Paulita's feelings, or those of the peasant girl in the tale, are hurt, the pain is redeemed by the beauty which results from it. This idea is one which argues for the justification of the means by the end. Though we do not know precisely how far Jarnés would have been willing to adhere to this principle, or whether he would have agreed that the end justifies the means in other than the artistic sphere, we can see a further development of this notion in something he wrote thirteen years after *Paula and Paulette*. In his biographical sketch of Stefan Zweig, Jarnés asked: "Are we at the end of that line of exemplary men who lived in misery and died in obscurity in order to leave us a poem, a cathedral, a symphony, a scientific law?"[17]

The pain and difficulties of life may be compensated for by the production of a work of art. In considering the work of art as the most valuable thing in life, Jarnés believed that its successful achievement justified any suffering entailed in its production. He also assumed that the artist, the poet, the composer, do suffer in the pursuit of their art. Perhaps the assumption is based on personal experience; perhaps it merely shows a certain Romantic residue in his conception of the artist. For Jarnés, the artist is almost by definition a solitary sufferer.

The second chapter of the novel offers a justification of Brook's suicide. Brook, an editor of *The Times*, has lived his life to the full. A *bon vivant*, he was Paula's lover and thereby the betrayer of his partner, her husband. However, at one of his bacchanalian feasts with a group of prostitutes, he discovers that the signs of age have begun to alter his handsome face and to herald his approaching demise. He determines to take his own life to prevent others from witnessing his decline and death (p. 214). He says he had tried to spend his life "learning the most profound art on Earth, the art of laughing; but the spirit cannot laugh if there is nothing left in the heart but ashes" (p. 205).

Brook exemplifies Jarnés' view of art as the province of the young, and of art as young in itself. Brook's aging and his impending physical decline signal a contradiction: art, humor, and grace cannot exist in the old and sick. Brook would rather kill himself at the first signs of old age than live on incapable of laughter and of producing the inventive and humorous histories with which he populated the Abbey's grottoes. Some of his inventions and notes, written down in his notebooks, pass on to Julio at his death; among them, notes on Viviana and Merlín which will become the legend of the same name which Jarnés published in 1930.

Julio tells us that with his notebooks Brook left "a robust vibration. His happiness, his thirst to fertilize every hour with a new eagerness, with a new idea, took hold of me" (p. 213). As in the case of Paulita, Julio views Brook as a pretext for his own artistic occupations. No lament, no disagreement with Brook's reasons for suicide arise to disturb the artistic profit Julio derives from interacting with Brook.

Again, we shall not say that Julio's attitude is inhuman. For to do so would be to endow Brook with a certain reluctance or anguish arising out of his decision to take his life. However, he approaches suicide with equanimity and even with relief. Brook is not, despite a superficial resemblance, another Dorian Gray, bent on prolonging his life of pleasure and terrified by the toll it takes on him. His death leaves no widow or small children bereft of their husband and father; his familial relations have been attenuated by their extra-marital quality. He is merely the carrier of an art which belongs to the young and healthy; when his health and youth fail, he passes his legacy on to Julio, amid the same happiness and inventiveness with which he had lived.

In the ending of the novel we have a certain mixing of real life and fiction. Brook's notebooks which he leaves to Julio contain the notes for *Vivien and Merlin*. Jarnés borrows these from his own character when he writes that legend in 1930. We should note that the mixing here is free of any element of confrontation between author and character. There is no clash of wills. Jarnés accepts what the characters, both Brook and Julio, give him, and continues in the same spirit the artistic rendering of beauty which they represented. Also, a confrontation between author and character is avoided because Jarnés appropriates Brook's notebooks for a legend which is not the novel *Paula and Paulette*.

Hence, the meeting of character and author occurs off-stage and is never concretely described.

IV   Locura y muerte de nadie
(The Madness and Death of Nobody)

Jarnés' fourth novel was published in 1929 also.[18] Contrary to his first three, *Locura y muerte de nadie (The Madness and Death of Nobody)* has a fairly well-developed plot line, several secondary characters who are more than shadows, and a thematic concern for a conspicuous social problem: the role of the individual in a mass society.[19]

Juan Sánchez is a man who feels himself to be without a personality. We first meet him waiting in a bank and resenting the anonymity enforced by the number which corresponds to his turn in line. We see him later as a faceless member of the rush-hour crowd at the end of the day. In continual rebellion against his role as mass-man, Juan attempts to assert himself one day in the plaza where newsreel cameramen are filming a crime. He manages to place himself directly in front of the cameras for a brief moment before the crowd of onlookers swells around him and blocks him out. When the newsreel is shown in the theater, however, Juan's features are blurred, and his hard-won moment in the camera's focus is swept away all too quickly by the equally blurred and swirling faces of the others in the crowd.

Juan is married to Rebeca who in turn is the mistress of Arturo, who knows her as Matilde. Arturo's motivation is the reverse of Juan's; he delights in losing his personality, in pretending that he can live the life of another man. When Rebeca, in the throes of passion, cries out the name of another, Arturo is immensely pleased. When Juan shows Arturo a nude painting of Rebeca, Arturo recognizes her as his Matilde. Thenceforth, even Juan's attempts to gain the personality of an outraged husband avenging his wife's infidelity are thwarted because Rebeca-Matilde and Arturo adroitly avoid giving him an opening in which to assert his husbandly honor.

Juan tries to find a personality for himself through music, poetry and painting, but he fails here as well because he has only a mediocre talent. His desperation leads him to welcome the idea of a personality gained through notoriety; accordingly, he plans and carries out the embezzlement of funds from his business. He keenly anticipates the discovery of the theft and its coverage in the newspapers where he will finally shine forth as a "personality." However, he is cheated of his goal even here, for the newspapers attribute the theft to his partner. Juan's end, entirely in keeping with the problem he embodies, comes about when he is run over by a truck and killed. The newspapers, in referring to the event, call him an unidentified pedestrian, and thereby rob him of even an obituary personality.

The novel is full of skilled descriptions of urban masses; Juan Sánchez is the perfectly alienated individual, searching fruitlessly for a means by which to endow his being with meaning. Although there is an echo here of Augusto Pérez in Unamuno's *Niebla*, the problems of both heroes are quite different. Pérez lives the major part of his fictional life without being concerned about existential or teleological matters. Only when he discovers that his creator intends to do away with him does he leap out of the mundane fictional plane to confront his destiny and, when he loses the ensuing struggle with Unamuno, to assert the Pyrrhic victory of his fictional immortality. Juan Sánchez' problem takes priority over Pérez', for he does not even have a personality in which to believe and with which to argue against a capricious creator for its extension in time.

Sánchez' relations with the other characters are, like those of the protagonists of Jarnés' first three novels, tangential and essentially empty of meaning. Although his wife, Rebeca, initially had a meaningful interaction with him, playing the Sancho to his Quixote, she soon enough gives him up emotionally to lose herself with her lovers Arturo and Alfredo. In the second edition, though not in the first, Arturo and Rebeca-Matilde do achieve a relationship more meaningful than the strictly sexual when Rebeca-Matilde arouses Arturo's jealousy and he declares that he loves her.

Sánchez' determined efforts to forge a personality for himself seem indeed quixotic for, from the fictional point of view, his personality is marked by the desire to have one. He disdains what he is in order to seek what he cannot be; that is his personality. In casting off the successive personalities which he achieves (mediocre painter, would-be jealous husband, embezzler, etc.), he resembles Alberto Díaz de Guzmán in Pérez de

Ayala's *La pata de la raposa* (1911). Alberto Díaz' rejection of the personality he has become leads him, however, to affirm his animal nature; he rejects the life of a cultured *señorito* so as to "animalize himself," that is, get into closer touch with his instinctual life.

For Sánchez, however, there is no higher or lower goal to reach. His problem essentially is that he refuses to accept himself as he is. Jarnés is writing under the influence of Ortega's *La rebelión de las masas* at a time when the problems of mass-society seem full of foreboding. The threat to culture and to an ordered political life offered by mass-man seemed especially grave to our author, whose professional life was dedicated to the exaltation of art and culture, to the praise of the sensibilities and intelligence of the individual.

In a way, then, Juan Sánchez' dilemma arises out of the conflict between his intelligence (which forces him to acknowledge that he is part of the masses) and his will (to differentiate himself from the masses). It might be objected that Jarnés has biassed the outcome by giving Sánchez enough perspective on himself to recognize his mediocrity; for one of the traits postulated about mass-man is precisely his inability to acknowledge his mediocrity, a blindness to recognize it. Real mass-man, by definition, is thought to be indifferent to his standing as a mass-man; indeed, he is thought by Ortega and others to exult in it.

Another objection we might make is that all of Sánchez' efforts aim at ending his mass-status; were they to succeed he should cease being a mediocrity and achieve novelistically heroic stature. Judging frim this novel, Jarnés seemed not to believe in that goal for Sánchez. Furthermore, such an outcome would place *The Madness and Death of Nobody* dangerously close to the "traditional" novel in which the hero faces adversity, struggles against it, and wins through to his just deserts. It is doubtful that Jarnés had this conception of the hero, novelistic or real, or that his view of the novel would admit such neat, "satisfying" novelistic structures. If, in addition, as Nora believes, *The Madness and Death of Nobody* presents something of Jarnés' own lived experience, then we can glimpse some of the author's self-doubt and pessimism.[20]

In the style of this novel, Jarnés continues to exploit techniques developed earlier: use of arithmetical notions to describe characters, perception of people as geometrical solids, and making human figures resemble and behave like machines.[21] As in his earlier work, also, these "dehumanizing" traits appear sporadically and are not sustained over the course of the novel, nor are they wholeheartedly espoused by Jarnés. Where in *Paula and Paulette* the protagonist is called "number 479" only to lose that designation when he and Paula meet and begin their relationship, Arturo, who is referred to as "number 351" while he is waiting in the bank, loses that designation when he begins to interact with Juan Sánchez. The perceptal frame through which the author sees a female form as a combination of cones, cylinders, and planes is only used intermittently to show a new perspective.

Furthermore, and most important, the geometrical frame is not imparted to the character as an inherent trait, but is rather like a lens which permits the author a temporary unique view of the character. To this extent, it is employed from outside the character as a way of handling details in a new way. That is why the characters are not described throughout the novel in geometric language, nor do they behave, except momentarily, as mechanized beings. Though the book is liberally endowed with what Ilie calls "dehumanizing" details, it is clear that Jarnés is not propounding "dehumanization" as an artistic method. For the use of those details is almost always intended to undercut the character, ridicule him, or present him in a novel—hence inherently worth-while aesthetically—aspect. Also, because Jarnés rejected systems and rigid logic, he was incapable of making a character bear "dehumanizing" traits entirely or over the course of a whole novel. The character had to display a certain freedom, to defy the application, by author or critic, of a unitary trait or set of traits throughout the book.

Our author's practice in this regard is similar to his use of myths in characterization. Just as he does not recreate any of the Classical myths at length, but rather invokes mythical figures intermittently, so he uses geometrical or mechanical language only intermittently in his characterizations. In addition, the "dehumanizing" traits he ascribes to his characters are not intended to carry any symbolic value except, at the most, the spontaneous and fleeting insight the author had into one discrete aspect of the characters. Nowhere in Jarnés do we find the dehumanization of Kafka's *Metamorphosis*, or the personifications of Barth's *Giles Goat-Boy*, nor, we need hardly add, the dehumanization and mechanization common in the characters of certain science fiction writers. Furthermore, the geometrical or mechanical characterizations in Jarnés do not evoke corresponding geometry or mechanism in the other characters. Where, for example, Cela can characterize Mrs. Caldwell with geometry (in his new preface to the definitive edition in his *Obra completa*), referring to her personality as an icosahedron, it is for the purpose of evoking a congruent solid figure in her son, in order to emphasize their spiritual unity. However, the geometry in the description of Paulita does not evoke any similar or contrasting geometry in Julio, although because of the attraction Julio feels for her, it might easily have done so.

In general, Jarnés can be seen to deplore the mechanization of modern life and the progressive automation of human beings. His censure of these trends, in line with Ortega's, is what endows Juan Sánchez' predicament with its pathos, as well as a healthy portion of the ridiculous. Far from allying himself with the forces of dehumanization in modern life, Jarnés took a firm stand against them.

V Teoría del zumbel
(Theory of the Top-String)

In *Teoría del zumbel (Theory of the Top-String)* we are offered a fictional elaboration of certain notions Jarnés held about the wholeness of man, and art's responsibility to depict all facets of man's life.[22] In five chapters, a prologue and an epilogue, the author relates the adventures and misadventures of a rather directionless young man named Saulo, heir to the banking fortune of Casa Bermúdez. The novel's episodes are designed to illustrate the theories Jarnés set forth in its prologue, "Bajo el signo de cáncer."

The prologue begins with a statement which is a variation on Ortega's dictum about the present-day need for psychology in fictional characterizations (see pp. 42-43 above). Continuing Ortega's line of thought, Jarnés says that every artist carries within him a mirror which may be focussed outward and/or inward. If he looks outward, what the artist produces will enrich the general history of mankind; if inward, he will enrich the monograph of his own spirit. "Today it is very difficult for a work of art to be produced which will not make a certain contribution to that monograph" (p. 10).

Jarnés quotes Jung's *The Unconscious* on the essential nature of man's irrational side, and agrees with the latter's labelling the irrational element the "collective unconscious" (pp. 14-15). However, the young artists of the day seem not to want to develop a personal and unique style; they seem to be tending toward "a noxious impersonality" (p. 17). Again, as he was to do so often, Jarnés stigmat zes the "impersonalism" (i.e., dehumanization) of the young writers and artists of his day, as well as the schools of art which at that time proliferated under the banners of one "ism" or another. Jarnés advances a clear censure of Surrealism on exactly this basis; for if a writer follows André Breton's thinking, he will become, unless he is truly a writer of genius, merely a writer for the masses, a writer without style (p. 19).

Then, in remarks which are probably simpler than the subject demands, Jarnés asserts the complexity of man, and the duty of art to reflect and depict all of man in all his states of being: man in his earthly concerns, man reaching upward ("the superman"), and man rooted in his unconscious ("the sub-man") (p. 27). There had been precedent and example enough in Western art and literature for the depiction of man in his earthly and his spiritual quests. And too, modern psychological studies have revealed in artists and authors from the past sophisticated and detailed portrayals of man's unconscious life. The new element added by the psychologists of the irrational and the abnormal, Freud at their head, was the decisive influence on man's existence of his unconscious life. Here, Jarnés enters a *caveat*: "Nor should we chart our course, like the persistent Freudian, through the disturbed riches of dreams, muddied by subterranean currents of dubious and at times foul-smelling origin" (pp. 28-29). Viewing himself as the captain of his ship of literature, Jarnés defends against the eddies and tides which may influence the direction of his ship. We are quite at a loss to explain Jarnés apparent distaste for abnormal psychology. Clearly however, he was both attracted to and repelled by it, for in the passage just quoted, he symbolically assumes the role of Odysseus bravely refusing to succumb to the blandishments ("the disturbed riches") of the sirens.[23]

Art should never restrict itself to the depiction of only "one-third of man," either unconscious man, earthly man, or spiritual man; but it should present all three men in a harmonious fusion, fully articulated and whole: "The triple man, entire, host of impulses. Something more than a whole man" (p. 31). In what strikes us as a minor quibble, Jarnés takes aim at Unamuno's well-known *hombre de carne y hueso,* the man of flesh and blood who is "a whole man." The disagreement between the two authors is more apparent than real, however, because Jarnés does not really depart from Unamuno's conception of character, except in certain superficial ways, e.g., lack of continuity in the novelistic action. Can we say that Unamuno ignores one or another aspect of Jarnés' "triple man" in his portraits of Augusto Pérez or of Tía Tula? We see their tri-faceted natures with more coherence than we would in Jarnés because Unamuno's novels tell more of a story than Jarnés'. Jarnés' comments, in any case, are more directly aimed at the Surrealists than at Unamuno. Their main thrust is to reclaim for the fictional character some of the well-roundedness and complexity which had been stripped away by Surrealism and by novelists of other vanguard persuasions, "dehumanizers" among them.

The plot of *Theory of the Top-String* revolves around the efforts made by two opposing groups to secure the banking fortune of Saulo Bermúdez for their own interests. On one side stand Padre Valdivia and Julia, spiritual guide and sister respectively of the heroine, Blanca. Julia's ambition is to redeem Saulo from a life of lechery and thereby induce him to leave his millions to the Church. She is willing to use her sister in this project, despite the fact that Blanca has grown to womanhood in a convent and would undoubtedly reject the plan if she knew its underlying motives. Blanca, under Valdivia's zealous guardianship, hadn't the slightest knowledge of love; in fact, "she still believed that babies came from Paris" (p. 39).

Opposing Julia and Valdivia is Doctor Carrasco, a reincarnation of the Cervantine Carrasco, whose ambition it is to arrange a match between Saulo and the daughter of the wealthy Gutiérrezes. For Carrasco knows what the other characters do not: the Bermúdez fortune has been dissipated by Saulo's lavish style of life. Practical man that he is, Carrasco wants to cement the remains of Saulo's fortune with that of Fundición Gutiérrez.

At the spa where Blanca has met Saulo, Julia decides to enlist three people in her plan for their marriage. The first member of this "junta" is Padre Valdivia, who will speak for man's spiritual side. Second is the spa's physician representing earthly man. The third member of the board is to be the novelist himself, speaking for the unconscious side of man. However, in what by this point in our study we have seen to be a habitual disclaimer of an active role, Jarnés protests against joining the group in their plan: "I don't want to belong to any 'junta' for the reparation of lives" (p. 56). He says he will observe the deceitful activities of Valdivia and Julia, will write his diary, and will turn his back on all the "subterranean manipulations."

If the pretenders to Saulo's presumed fortune are criticized for their deceit, Carrasco, on the other hand, is criticized for the pedestrian nature of his ambition. Saulo at one point says to the author that he wants to "cheer Blanca up" [*alegrarla*]. The author corrects him: "You mean excite her" [*inquietarla*]. Saulo retorts: "Excitement is the same as happiness" (p. 57). The two are really spokesman for Jarnés in the exposition of one of his favorite themes: happiness as an elusive, unsettling, disrespectful but necessary ingredient of life. Later, commenting on how common Carrasco is, how average and uninspired he is in word and deed, Jarnés says: "For all the disturbances [*inquietudes*] of the spirit he has found an ungainly Greek name—how far Greek has fallen from Pindar to Freud!" (p. 73). Of course, we ought to point out that in critizing Carrasco's Freudianism—especially since he has made Carrasco a symbol of the mediocre and unintelligent—Jarnés is setting up a straw man. For everyone would agree that the oversimplifiers of Freud have only obscured the useful clinical benefits of his psychology. Nonetheless, as a jibe at those oversimplifiers, the comment is well placed.

Carrasco wages his campaign in favor of the Gutiérrez girl so effectively that Saulo seems on the point of giving up Blanca. At this point, the author puts aside the passive role of mere observer: "I cannot tolerate an impertinent detour in the novel. Saulo must remain completely free to pursue his path as a hero" (pp. 88-89). Although the act here seems Unamunian enough, we should realize that Jarnés' interest is not in coming to grips with his hero in open combat. Nor is Carrasco an opponent of sufficient stature. Rather, Jarnés wants to protect his hero from Carrasco's undue suasion, leaving Saulo apparently free to choose his own fate. He is Saulo's guardian angel, where Unamuno was Pérez' avowed antagonist.

In following his path as hero, Saulo seduces Blanca, just before his return to the city to face his financial disaster. The seduction is described this way: "They go through all the plastic positions by means of which love usually holds itself back. First, standing, in the middle of the office; then, seated on the edge of the sofa; finally lying together, victorious . . ." (p. 163). In this scene we have a series of pictorial attitudes, separate, static and, we might say, sculptural. The seduction might have been written from a cinematic point of view, for each separate stage is actually a still shot.

Yet the author's delight is at least equally vested in the seduction as in the contemplation of each successive posture of the lovers. As in Paulita's bending over to pick up the apples (see pp. 74-75 above), Jarnés wants to isolate parts of what a more traditional novelist would treat as a smoothly flowing, unitary action, in order to reveal to the reader new (inéditas) sources of aesthetic pleasure. The adverbs ("first, then, finally") link the scenes together as a scenarist's directions might do in a movie. The seduction remains a coherent unified action, but merely stopped at three points for closer contemplation by the artist and his readers.

The technique of stopping the action which we see here is in an early stage of its development. Once unified actions are broken into their components, these may be rearranged at will and interspersed with other actions with which they have no relationship. The splitting up of actions in this manner will be more fully developed as a technique by novelists in the 1950's and 1960's, e.g., Cela (La colmena), Carpentier (El acoso), and Fuentes (La muerte de Artemio Cruz), to mention only three who wrote in Spanish.

We should not overstate the cinematic analogy, however, for Jarnés' technique is still well within the novelist's province. Although he separates the seduction into three "still" scenes, he does not rearrange them in sequence, nor place them in any other contexts in the novel. They do not recur elsewhere in the novel, nor are they made symbolic of broader themes or actions in the book. In addition, although the camera's eye is usually considered objective, in that after being aimed and focussed it takes in whatever is before it, Jarnés' view of the seduction is highly selective. He does not in fact provide much detail for the scene, preferring to let the reader do this. Thus, as much as we might be tempted to call the technique "dehumanized" or even worse, "dehumanizing," we ought to remember that, far from being mechanized or depersonalized, Blanca and Saulo are being portrayed in what the author considered the highest human medium, that of the aesthetically skilled and pleasing portrait. And in the final phrase, "lying together, victorious," we do not see depersonalization but rather a joyous, eminently human and personal act of love.

Upon leaving Blanca, Saulo meets with an auto accident, and before he dies experiences a phantasmagoric dream in which his father and grandfather appear to him, reproaching him for having squandered the Bermúdez fortune. An old patient in the clinic where Saulo is taken believes himself to be God, and explains the meaning of the novel's title to Saulo: "Every human life is a top which I throw to the ground. The top spins as long as the spirit moves it; the impulse is measured by the length of the string. I contemplate with sadness these disorderly lives which chose a string as short as yours, Saulo" (p. 200). "God" shows Saulo a chest full of top-strings, some long like Methuselah's, others short like Bécquer's. Saulo sees his own there and protests that he's not dead yet. When he further protests against his impending death, "God" tells him not to blaspheme. "God" says that if "He" still had the power of the thunderbolt, he would kill Saulo (pp. 206-7). The Unamunian echoes again are obvious. But Jarnés' God is, like the author himself, more passive than Unamuno's. Saulo's "string runs out" and he dies.

The epilogue seems a throwback to an earlier novelistic tradition, for in it Jarnés tells us what happened to Blanca. Blanca had borne Saulo's son, spending the last three months of her pregnancy in Switzerland, and marrying Carrasco. At the end of the epilogue, in a scene which because of its obviousness seems rather heavy-handed, we see Blanca's and Saulo's son, Pedro, spinning a top: "The child returns to his game. . . . The top con-

tinues spinning as long as the childish—and divine—whim lasts"
(p. 252).

VI Escenas junto a la muerte
(Scenes on the Brink of Death)

Jarnés' sixth novel was published in 1931.[24] Like the novels
which came before it, *Escenas junto a la muerte (Scenes on the
Brink of Death)* lacks any chronological plot action. Rather, as
were *The Useless Professor* and *Theory of the Top-String*, most
notably, it is a set of vignettes having the protagonist and one
or two minor characters in common. The vignettes cohere somewhat better here because they are unified by an even tone of
frustration, despair, and pessimism. Although Jarnés' bleak vision
is relieved a bit in the fourth tale by the interpolation of an
account of a Chaplin movie, the humor in the other tales is
ironic, bitter, and sometimes black.

The book begins with the hero in despair over his studies for
the competitive examinations for a teaching post, and contemplating suicide. Leaning over the edge of the roof of his building, he
gives a succinct description of the world as he sees it: "Below,
the night keeps making its puppets dance." The puppets are:
Faust trying to square the circle; a student cramming a syllabus
on which he will not be tested; a whore for the seventh time
that evening stopping a penniless passerby; a dressmaker end-
lessly sewing a wedding dress for a woman whose fiancé is
impotent; the poet who finally hits upon the trite lines with which
to close his ode (pp. 10-11). All these human puppets, each a
tiny study in futility, crowd in upon the hero, convincing him
of the meaninglessness of life. The puppets are dancing the dance
of ultimate or incipient failure, that is, a prelude to the dance of
death, hence their appeal for and agreement with the hero's
mood. We learn some of the causes of his despair when he tells
us that things had lost their meaning: "They were all the same
to me, a world war, the anguish of a mute nightingale, the
death of a pope, the silence of a suckling lamb on the way to
slaughter, a railway disaster, the astonishment of a street urchin
in front of a candystore window" (p. 14).

The levelling out of meaning in his life began when the hero
discovered his own limits: "One day, I was horrified to find myself imprisoned in the stone cell of my inexorable definition. I was

slowly becoming hardened" (p. 15). With an echo of the same despair with which Unamuno was wont to protest against the omnipresent categorizations of things, Jarnés has prepared his hero for suicide. The suicide is prevented, however, by the intervention of the hero's fellow competitor, and the ensuing narratives are the flashbacks the hero relates to him.

The five tales which make up the novel are simple accounts of the hero's experiences with three women, Juno, Isabel, and a married woman whom he calls Elvira de Pastrana. Juno, whose real name is Aurora, seeks to provoke her sweetheart to jealousy by having him discover her talking to the narrator. Her *novio* strikes her, and when the narrator leaps to her defense, the outraged lover falls against a chair without the narrator's having struck him. The narrator thenceforth is proclaimed a heroic defender of womankind although he neither pretended to nor deserved such fame.

The second tale takes the narrator on an anguished nighttime search of someone who will aid him in his distress; he believes he has suffered a heart attack from excessive aimless studying. He meets Isabel, a girl from the provinces who is the mistress of a marquis, who takes pity on him because she believes him to be suffering from a disappointment in love. In the third tale, the narrator, who is employed at the post office, saves a married woman from the possible wrath of her jealous husband. The woman has been receiving letters regularly from her lover who addresses them to Elvira de Pastrana. One day, she comes to call for her mail with her suspicious husband who is certain he will discover her infidelity. The narrator, however, does not give her the letters which had arrived for her and the husband is deprived of the chance to vent his jealousy. In return for his astuteness, the narrator receives a grateful smile from Elvira.

When we turn to some of the structural matters in these episodes, we note a common theme: love as a fleeting pastime incapable of enduring. Also, we find that, as is true of all of Jarnés' heroes, our narrator refuses to play a heroic role. He is diffident and perturbed at the reputation he gains in the encounter with Juno's jealous boyfriend, for he knows he played no hero's role. The narrator passes through each of the stories, as it were aimlessly, touching other characters, even becoming involved in their lives (e.g., when he sets about bringing Isabel out of her illiteracy). But soon he loses interest in the other, or events intervene to separate them, and nothing is left save memory and the motive for another vignette.

In *Scenes on the Brink of Death* Jarnés seems to·have divested his prose of even those few novelistic elements which had remained in it. There is no development of character, for the book is a series of flashbacks to discrete episodes; when the narrator reappears in successive tales, he is not a more mature character novelistically, nor does he seem to have incorporated his fictional experiences. Whether Jarnés had been hampered in the writing of this book by some personal crisis, or whether his determination to write novels which would be as different as he could make them from those other novelists had written, we do not know.[25]

Jarnés' writing has not, however, lost its humor. The "useless professor's" explanation of the alphabet to Isabel calls forth her ingenuous reactions. In her naiveté, she responds to literacy with some of the irreverence of the *greguerías* of Gómez de la Serna. We learn, for example, that the full stop "is the little drop of mercury in the thermometer of style" (p. 187). The *greguería* appears again in the exclamation points which are like telegraph poles (p. 188). The illiterate Isabel is an apt vehicle for the author's notion that the innocent, especially children, are endowed with special artistic powers.

In this work we also find several instances of Jarnés' use of mythological figures to endow his characters with a personality. For example, during their lessons in literacy and love, the narrator and Isabel are chaperoned by Isabel's maid, Justina: "Justina represents the law. Like a mythological dragon she guards in the name of the marquis the now quivering flesh of my Andromeda" (p. 136). The mythological note should not be over-interpreted, for to do so would be to make our passive anti-hero into Andromeda's lover, Perseus. The narrator is not even fleetingly a Perseus in this work. As we saw above (pp. 59-61), the use of mythology is not sustained or reasoned out. Jarnés was not rewriting the myths; he was postulating their survival intact from ancient times to his own day.

Jarnés continues in this work to make use of highly concrete language, often using metaphors derived from modern technology. He protests, in a tone which Ortega might have used, against the fast pace of modern life. For if the speed of the automobile has done away with fatigue in the traveller it has also deprived him of the chance to rest and contemplate his surroundings (p. 184). In *Scenes on the Brink of Death*, indeed, the language serves the predominantly sombre tone. "Death is locked up within us like the negative current in a cable" (p. 205).

VII Lo rojo y lo azul (The Red and the Blue)

In 1932 Jarnés' seventh novel was published.[26] *Lo rojo y lo azul (The Red and the Blue)*, subtitled "Homenaje a Stendhal" ("Homage to Standhal"), takes the hero, Julio (namesake of the hero of Stendhal's *The Red and the Black*), to Barcelona where in three chapters he is inducted into the Army, becomes involved with the middle-class Cecilia, and takes part in an unsuccessful barrack coup. The novel's epigraph reads: "In Homage / 1831-1931 / To You, My Old Friend Stendhal / On the Hundredth Anniversary / of / Your Inimitable / JULIEN SOREL."[27]

Julio, like other Jarnesian protagonists with the same name, shares with Julien Sorel a lack of direction and of a respectable background. Julio was a "fugitive from a priest-factory. Orphaned and with no fortune. Alone in the world" (p. 10). But where the Stendhalian namesake makes his way with a certain force and opportunism, Julio does not want to "arrive."

On the train to Barcelona Julio meets Guillermina who tells him her neatly formulated plans for the future: a comfortable marriage and the untroubled routine of the bourgeoise. Jarnés says Guillermina's plan was "very clear; therefore [it was] so doubtful. Julio's seemed excessively obscure; therefore, it was so human" (p. 18). Julio, expressing Jarnés' position, views the predictable and settled routine of the middle class as a kind of death. Life was to be found elsewhere, in the impetuous acceptance of life's contingencies, and in the affirmation of the unexpected.

Both Julio and Guillermina go to Barcelona to seek a new life. Julio is reborn when, for the medical examination at his induction, he gets undressed and joins the slow-moving file of the other naked recruits (p. 23). Guillermina, as the train arrived in Barcelona, had put on fresh makeup; Julio thought her repaired beauty "a trivial resurrection" (p. 19). Although both characters begin life in the city as "new-borns," neither finds success or satisfaction. Guillermina's plans for marriage fall through, and

she is even rejected for a job as a chorus girl because her legs
are too thin (p. 89).

Julio's experience in the army serves only to convince him of
the evils of military life. The first proof of this comes when he
enters the barracks: "It was then that he was turned into a
number, a tactical element" (p. 21).[28] Barracks life is responsible
for the crushing effacement of the recruits' personalities; it turns
the men into automata. But beyond this, it enables Julio to see
his fellows reduced to their human minimum: "You haven't really
begun to despise humanity until you've seen, as now, so many
men together in the nude" (p. 25). The army is not at fault, of
course, for the men's appearance. But with a pronounced Orteguian tone, the author scorns them. From this initial point of
view of men as inherently repellent, we progress to other more
subtle reasons for Julio's rejection both of men in the mass and
of the military. Chief among these is the hypocrisy in the claim
that the army serves the needs of the nation; for Julio, the army
merely serves to advance the thirst for power of those in
command.

Julio's life in the barracks is bleak indeed. An inept trainee, he
cannot learn to march correctly, for he is usually distracted by
the passage of a pretty girl, or by his own fantasies while march-
ing. One day at reveille, he imagines that Diana has blown the
bugle call on her hunting horn. Then he pictures her running
naked through the barracks among the men who are putting on
their uniforms: "Julio went on getting dressed. Diana had
disappeared, and where he had just seen the pink tips of her
breasts there now stupidly arose the bristly moustaches of the
corporal" (pp. 44-45). This fantasy, artful and humorous, is an
example of a sort of cinematic imagination. For a director would
merge the breasts of Diana into the corporal's moustache with
a lap dissolve. By recourse to this sort of distraction, Julio
relieves some of the tedium of his training.

In the second section of the novel, Julio meets Cecilia Pala-
frugell who works in her family's stationery store. He is initially
charmed by her and soon their relations seem to point to matrimony. Cecilia's family sees in Julio a promising addition to the
staff of their business. Cecilia's attraction for him is partly due
to the fact that she seems to share the romantic aspect of the
gaudy and saccharine post cards on sale in the store. He calls

her his "Circe," and she is his major distraction from the boredom of military life. Eager to learn a useful trade, Julio applies to the academy of Braulio Martínez, hopeful of gaining a chance for "a future" (p. 82).

But Braulio wants to know about his past, and his experience. Since Julio has left the seminary he considers that he has no past worthy of mention. Without a past he cannot have "a future." Braulio's inquiries into his past soon end, and he begins to give Julio a political indoctrination; Braulio has for years been a propagandist for Communism.

Julio receives Braulio's political lessons with sympathy but without real conviction. Braulio is a kind of "useless professor" for Julio, since the Communist teachings with which he enlivens their accounting lessons avail him not at all. For many years, Braulio has been distributing clandestine Marxist pamphlets, all the while expecting to be arrested. And he has so far failed to "convert" Julio that the attempted coup in the final chapter fails because of Julio's lack of revolutionary fervor.

Julio decides to break with Cecilia because he feels increasingly reluctant to assume the monotonous life of the good bourgeois. One day, Julio sees a casket being carried out of Cecilia's house. He insists to Rubí, Cecilia's friend, that Cecilia has died, when in fact she has not. Using the money with which he was going to pay for his accounting lessons, he takes Rubí out, thus severing his relations with Cecilia, the business world, and the comfortable future which awaited him.

In structural terms, he breaks with Cecilia because of his progressive assimilation of Marxist, anti-bourgeois thinking. However, because he does not espouse Marxism with the requisite discipline or fervor, his rejection of the bourgeois life does not lead him to a full acceptance of the Marxian alternative. The hero's action here is structurally similar to that of Julio's conduct in *The Paper Guest*. There, Estrella contended against the seminary for Julio's allegiance, but, leaving the seminary did not direct Julio to a whole-hearted or permanent acceptance of the alternative, life with Estrella.

In the last section of the novel, Julio takes part in a conspiracy at the San Luis barracks. Julio's part in the rebellion is to take and hold the powder magazine, even if he must kill to do so. Not at all infused with the revolutionary zeal of his barracks mates, he tells us: "I can see that I am going to be *useless* to the cause of the disinherited, which is also my own" [italics added] (p. 197). And, in fact, he cannot shoot a lieutenant who intervenes at the height of the coup; thus, the coup is put down. Julio is not punished for his part in the rebellion, because the lieutenant promises out of gratitude not to report him.

After his failure to kill the lieutenant, Julio is hospitalized because of a nervous breakdown. He ponders his failure and concludes that he is a neurotic, thus of no value to women, and of scant value for men: "The neurotic may be a momentary hero, in those crises where suicide presents itself as a pleasure; but he is incapable of lasting heroism, of any useful persistence" (pp. 234-35). The lieutenant visits him, and by way of consoling him tells him that no revolutionary movement can succeeed without bitter hatred to fuel the fires of revolt. The lieutenant provides a sort of moral to the tale by telling him that generosity, or as some call it, cowardice, is the opposite of hatred. We should take refuge in our mutual generosity as it is "the only fruitful religion" (p. 236).

Because it resumes Julio's story at the point where he leaves the seminary, *The Red and the Blue* may be considered a sequel to *The Paper Guest*.[29] Novelistically, the work lacks a continuous plot action, continuity of scene, and well-rounded characters, as do the other novels. Like them too, it is full of digressions of a didactic sort; in this instance, of Marxist political thought. Perhaps we can see in this work a certain influence of the political situation in Spain in the 1930's although here as always, Jarnés is far from espousing any specific doctrine. He shunned "isms" in his life as well as in his art. The novel provides a kind of confrontation between revolutionary ideas and the status quo.

Julio, having left the seminary, and thoroughly disgusted with the military, is likewise incapable of adherence to a revolutionist's cause. Rather than retreat into a neutral position between the contending forces, he espouses a "doctrine" which appeals to neither side: mutual generosity as the only fruitful religion. This novel comes the closest in all of Jarnés' work to meeting the demands of a socially committed literature. It offers in capsule form a vision of some of the political and social convulsions which surrounded the fall of the monarchy in 1931, and which beset the Second Republic. It contains strong criticisms, founded in the author's liberal humanitarianism, of the major factors involved in those convulsions: the Army, the Church, the conservative middle class, and the partisans of the revolutionary Left.

And yet, Jarnés' idea of what a novel should be could not allow him to devote systematic attention either to the evolution of those social and political difficulties, nor to their concrete details. The discontinuities in the action, for example, prevent the reader from seeing characters in an ongoing struggle with or against political forces and events. The absence of solid secondary characters deprives the reader of the chance to perceive the author's opinion of how social conflicts arise and may be solved. Julio is given us, *a priori*, as a detached and almost unconcerned observer, like his Stendhalian namesake. He has rejected his past, and he rejects several different futures which present themselves. He exists in the present only, an ahistorical, apolitical, and asocial character.

To the extent that Julio is only a momentary Marxist or a half-hearted one, he resembles those of Jarnés' characters who are endowed momentarily with traits analogous to those of mythical figures. In the case of the mythical characteristics ascribed to his heroes and heroines, we saw that it was impossible to find a single myth recreated entirely in the novel. We found it fruitless to identify other characters in the novel with traits corresponding to those found in other characters in the myth, because the author had not given us a coherent reworking of the myth. In the case of this Julio also, our attempts to provide a fully-rounded fictional context for his political awareness are frustrated because Jarnés does not provide any coherent or fully-functioning characters whose politcal involvements might interact with Julio's. There are no well-rounded coconspirators, no wholeheartedly and obnoxiously bourgeois antagonists. Both in the details of characterization as well as in the structure of the novel as a whole, Jarnés stops short of providing thoroughgoing analogies to other areas of human experience. He refuses to make his characters or the trajectories they follow symbolic of anything.

Though he shares with his French forebear a loathing of poverty (p. 127), and a resentment of his insignificant place in the social scale (p. 124), Julio lacks Sorel's capacity to conform. So, where a marriage to Cecilia would abolish his poverty, he cannot bear the thought of a commercial career. And where he would gain a hero's acclaim by shooting the lieutenant, he cannot feel the necessary degree of hatred. He is in the same place at the end of the novel as he was at the beginning in terms of his fictional trajectory. Unfortunately, there is no sequel to *The Red and the Blue,* and we are prevented from further speculation about his fate.

VIII   *Minor Novelistic Works*

In this section we consider briefly certain books of Jarnés' which, either because of their more modest pretension or the circumstances of their publication, seem to us less important for an appreciation of his overall contribution to the Spanish novel.

Salón de estío (Summer Salon), a collection of four loosely related short stories, appeared in 1929.[30] What unites the four is a thread of ironic deflation which makes the stories and particularly the characters in them ridiculous. The four tales are "Andromeda," written in 1926 and dedicated to Antonio Espina, "Circe," written in 1927 and dedicated to Ernesto Giménez Caballero, "Folletín," written in 1928, and "Película," written, we may assume, in 1929. "Circe" is the primitive version of the second section of *The Red and the Blue;* in the initial version the story was forty-seven pages long; by 1932, when it was included in the novel, it had grown, by the addition of basically descriptive material, to one hundred pages.

The third and fourth stories in the book aim at making the excess of amorous passion seem foolish. "Película" is a brief recreation of the story of Romeo and Juliet. It recounts Romeo's attempt to reach his beloved's window by climbing up a rope. He falls to the ground—an echo of Calisto's fall outside Melibea's garden in the *Celestina*—and Juliet begins to descend the rope to comfort him. The canon of the manor comes upon her and makes her retreat to her room, whereupon a family imbroglio ensues. Juliet promises to give up her lover. When she awakens the next day at dawn, she is horrified at the previous night's events, and throws herself from the window—another Celestine echo, this of Melibea's leap to her death from a tower—where a Civil Guard catches her in his arms and takes her to the police station.

"Folletín" tells of an outraged husband who comes to grief

when he gives vent to his jealousy of his wife's lover. The Lover and the Perfidious Wife are surprised *in flagrante delicto;* the husband draws a gun and forces them, still in the nude, out of the room. The wife falls down four flights of stairs to her death, whereupon the police impound the nude painting of the wife which the lover had been working on at the time. Jarnés says the truth of the crime lies in the painting rather than in the wife's own physical beauty, for the painting, because it is art, is a higher truth.

The lover, gone mad, spends his time painting stairways and believing his mistress is about to appear on his canvasses. After hearing the evidence in the case, the judge acquits the painting of guilt in causing the husband's jealousy, and sends it to the painter in the madhouse. Seeing the "truth" reappear, the painter regains his sanity, and seeking to make his fortune, sells a copy of it to the husband who thinks he has bought the original. When the latter realizes the deceit, he rips the painting to shreds with a knife, thus destroying the "truth" as he had previously destroyed his wife.

In both these stories, Jarnés ridicules the Romantic pose, with that criticism of the unrestrained passions which marked so much of his work. He also asserts the primacy of the created art object over its real-life inspiration. The feeling which pervades both tales is one of the ultimate futility of the irrational and impulsive action. As is true of Jarnés' characters generally, these characters are anti-heroic, not so much because they refuse to act out their heroic instincts, but precisely because they do. Jarnés implies that more could be gained, and a great deal less lost, by the application of reason.

"Circe" has been dealt with above in its extended version in *The Red and the Blue.* Little is to be gained in this study by cataloguing the variations between both versions. In "Andromeda" we come upon a story which can be considered typical of Jarnés' handling of chartcter, both male and female, and of novelistic action. Again, the plot line is spare and anecdotal, relating Julio Aznar's discovery of Elena Fourment tied naked to a tree in an olive grove. He rescues her, wraps her in a blanket, and takes her back to Augusta [Zaragoza]. There, he drives from store to store buying her a new wardrobe. When Elena is dressed and has applied her makeup (in a scene prefigured by

Guillermina in *The Red and the Blue*), Julio recognizes her as Carmela, an exotic dancer from the Parisiana Theater.

When Julio first comes upon Elena, he is in the midst of a nocturnal walk in which he is contemplating the delights of nature. He is loath to untie her because he doesn't want to plunge "into the labyrinth of action" (p. 20). Perhaps as a defense against his own potential erotic proclivities, Julio thinks Elena's naked body devoid of sexual stimulus. He rather thinks that all her capacities for "erotic suggestiveness" have remained in her stolen dress (p. 22).

On the ride back to the city, Elena, newly named Star by Julio, deprived of her own clothing and cosmetic adornment, tries to appear as coquettish and attractive as she can in the blanket which covers her. Julio, however, fails to succumb; in fact, when because of the bumpy road, the blanket slips and bares part of her body, he tenderly replaces it (pp. 36-37). In this episode, full of erotic and amorous possibilities, Jarnés restricts his hero to the role given him by his occupation. Julio is a surveyor, and in Star's shapely body under the blanket he sees, not a sexual invitation, but only a topographical map in the scale of 1:25,000 (p. 38).

In a passage which reveals a good deal about Jarnés' own fictional method, Julio says: "My profession [of surveyor] only obliges me to set limits, to fix bench marks and lay out boundaries. The content is left for the peasant, the poet and the painter" (p. 45). Likewise, what interests Julio and Jarnés in this fictionally pregnant situation is to tread the margins of it—Julio's antiheroic rescue, his preparations for their return to the city, his careful abstention from claiming Star's body as the legitimate prize of his heroism—rather than to fill it up with a common novelistic content. Such a content would include a seduction, the possible establishment of amatory ties between the two, and a suitable resolution to their encounter.

Our author holds Julio back from any of the expected actions. Hence, he produces an original situation with materials as old as literature itself. We may assume, judging from the third and fourth stories in the book, that Jarnés would have scorned an active sexual involvement on Julio's part because of its inevitable and overblown Romanticism, and its potentially bourgeois resolution. Instead, the restraint Julio displays allows him to draw a unique situation which is, we should admit, not without its own humor.

When Star is finally clothed and made up, and Julio recognizes her as a well-known strip-tease dancer, whose stage name is Carmela, she tells him her made-up face is not her real one but her stage face. Julio objects: "The only one. Because it is the only one which you have constructed. The other [face] is nothing but a vulgar inheritance" (p. 52). Julio is denigrating inheritance or, in literary terms, tradition, in order to exalt the results of Star's individual workmanship. Jarnés likewise discounts tradition so as to stress novelty and originality.

In the case of *Viviana y Merlín: leyenda (The Legend of Vivien and Merlin)*, we have less to do with a novel than with a retelling of the Arthurian tale, a retelling liberally dosed with Jarnés' ideas and digressions on àrt, the role of humor in art, and the opposition between the flesh and the spirit.[31] In addition, we find some comments akin to those in *Theory of the Top-String* (see pp. 83-84 above), on the need for an integralist view of man. King Arthur's Court is "a concentration of the energies of the soul in a battle against the fierce appetites of the flesh, its traditional enemy" (p. 18). In the king's court, however, the passions are dominated by the spirit. Merlín, the aged sage, is subject to the continual blandishments and seductiveness of Viviana who, in comments which could equally pertain to Jarnés' view of fiction, tells him: "You have to keep making love come alive every minute" (p. 62).

Merlín at length admits to his having ignored his instinctual life in order to concentrate only on his mind. He has done this because he thinks the passions are "not the product of delightfully harmonized vehemence" (p. 85). Viviana succeeds in teaching him how to harmonize the body and the spirit. Rather than seeing Viviana as a threat to Merlín, Jarnés sees her as the necessary contributor of grace and humor. He takes issue with one of his sources for this book—Tennyson in his *Idylls of the King*—and faults the Englishman for calling Vivien a false and crafty snake (p. 111).

Where Jarnés' Merlín feels Viviana to be a threat to his life of abstract thought, and the discovery of laws and formulas, his Viviana asks if it isn't much more human to formulate doubts than laws (p. 136). Again, as in the beginning of *The Red and the Blue,* we see Jarnés' opposition to the rigidities of laws and abstractions; and we see his affinity with Unamuno in the prestige he confers on the vital effectiveness of doubt. Jarnés had a continued, almost constitutional aversion to logic and systems. Hence, those of his characters who espouse or embody doubts, who manage to defeat logic, are always shown in a favorable light. The author's aversion explains why his novels do not express any systematic "philosophy of life" or any pragmatic approach to the solution of social, political, or literary problems. Doubt does not function as a goad for the character to seek answers to his problem or those of his society. Doubt is rather a character trait, like timidity in his male heroes, or behavior similar to that of mythical figures in his females; doubt in his characters is productive only in the sense that it saves them from incorporating into their lives any of the more notorious "rigidities" which life offers them, e.g., the life of a priest or a soldier.

Viviana and Merlín are united at the end of the work, and they find the solution to the great problem of "how to harmonize force with humor and wisdom" (p. 146). Viviana embodies the author's ideal of an integrated vitalism, for her humor "is the clear and clean product of the spiritual retort, with the taste of the whole human factory: sex, heart and mind" (p. 156). Thus, the humorist is the true poet, and the only one who can combine completely the magnificent being "who vibrates between the earth and the sun: man" *(ibid.).*

The gist of this "legend" then, is the importance of human contact, love, and disappointment as against theoretical knowledge and laws. Although the work may strike us as precious, even effete, we doubt that it can serve to bolster a thesis of Jarnés' dehumanization. On the contrary, it is the embodiment of his humanistic and vitalist viewpoint in art and life.

La novia del viento (The Wind's Sweetheart) is an extension of the first story in *Summer Salon.*[32] In *The Wind's Sweetheart,* the first chapter is the tale of "Andromeda." The other two chapters aim at providing some sort of conclusion to the relationship between Julio Aznar, surveyor, and Elena-Star-Carmela, the strip-tease dancer he rescued from the olive grove.

The second story in *The Wind's Sweetheart,* "Epimetheus' Digression," is an essay on the novel which comments on the excellences of "Andromeda," chief among them the fact that the story doesn't end at the moment the hero has the heroine undressed (p. 67). Jarnés says that the "experts" praised his failure to give an ending to the episode, for it allowed the reader to collaborate with the author by making his own epilogue *(ibid.).* Jarnés sees one of the novelist's main gifts as the ability to draw the reader into the novel; because "Andromeda" is open-ended, the reader is free to imagine a conclusion for it.

This second section ends after some remarks on the necessity of a spiritual dimension in relations between man and woman. Jarnés writes that physical love is fleeting, merely superficial: "As if anything fundamental for human life could come out of mere physiology" (p. 76). Since he has been unable to enjoy any spiritual dimension in his previous affairs with women, Julio decides to close his life to love: "If the whirlwind of love comes along, I will intensify my cultivation of my own independence, to the extreme of never influencing the destinies of others" (p. 77). Again, the note of withdrawal in the male hero which, in the "Andromeda" of *Summer Salon* was only a partial one.

The third and final section of this novel is entitled "Brunhilde in Flames." It begins with Julio entering a dance in progress at his hotel. His exploits with Carmela the previous night have preceded him, although distorted by the chauffeur who drove them back to the city and who has spread a number of false tales about what Julio did in the car. At the dance, Julio meets Brunilda; she and her father, Don Blas, have rented a house at the edge of town. One day, Julio, Brunilda, and her father go for a walk up the hill called "La Novia del Viento," i.e., "The Wind's Sweetheart." On their return, Brunilda makes Julio show her the tree to which Carmela had been tied. She stands next to the tree and asks Julio what he would do if she reenacted the episode as Andromeda. Julio does not reply (p. 104).

A week later, Julio visits Brunilda and finds her studio filled with studies of nudes, all of them women who have posed for Brunilda with their faces covered. Julio agrees to go to Brunlida's show at the Summer Salon. He receives a letter from Carmela who, now that her boyfriend has left her, wants to see him again. He is about to go to her when Brunilda stops him by unveiling what she calls her masterpiece: it is the scene in the olive grove, but instead of Carmela, Brunilda is bound to the tree. She then seduces Julio who swears his love and promises never to leave her. The curious thing about *The Wind's Sweetheart* is that it contradicts Jarnés' own position as expressed in "Epimetheus' Digression." If the main virtue of the first "Andromeda" had been that the novelist had allowed the reader to imagine his own epilogue, the main defect of this work is that the reader cannot do so. Both because the affair of Brunlida and Julio comes at the end of the novel and, more important, because it represents a logical end to their fictional trajectories, any epilogue other than the one implicit in the novel would be out of place.

Of course, the author might have written a sequel in which Julio leaves Brunilda, just as he alters the implicit conclusions of "Andromeda" in *The Wind's Sweetheart*. But to our knowledge, no sequel exists. Hence, we are forced to conclude that, although Jarnés valued the open-ended novel with its demand for reader participation, by 1940 he had come to prefer a more finished form.

The last two works which will concern us are related to each other in a way similar to the two just discussed. *Venus dinámica (Dynamic Venus)*[33] incorporated three of the five chapters of the earlier *Don Alvaro o la fuerza del tino (Don Alvaro or the Power of Good Aim)*.[34] The latter novelette, all things considered, is a negligible work. The hero, Eulogio, has had his calling card stolen by Isabel's lover. But the latter leaves Isabel at the altar. Her father, Don Alvaro, discovers her affair, and goes to shoot Eulogio in order to avenge the blot on his daughter's honor. Isabel corrects his mistaken identification, but only after Alvaro, the true Calderonian, has fired a shot into the wall and been arrested.

Eulogio and Isabel then become friends. They go to Eulogio's favorite café where his encounter with Alvaro has become the topic of general gossip. Isabel contrasts Eulogio favorably with her vanished ex-lover, because the latter "refused to enter the drama. He didn't want to commit himself" (p. 46). In an epilogue, Jarnés confesses ignorance about what Isabel and Eulogio did in the car on the way to her hotel. But, he adds, they were married, and before the year was out took their new-born son to visit his grandfather who was serving a three-year term for armed assault.

In all, the story conforms well enough to the general outlines of the *novela rosa*, the love-novel sometimes attacked for its pornography, and uniformly deprecated by our author for the pecuniary motives which lay behind its creation. We may speculate on the direction Jarnés' novelism was taking if, in June of 1936, he had published this novel in a series not of the highest quality, whose aim was merely the entertainment of the reader. Without the intervention of the Civil War, Jarnés might well have continued at this level, leaving behind him the more ambitious works he had had published by Revista de Occidente, and Espasa-Calpe. However, the war put a stop to this incipient decline by causing his exile and a host of new problems and demands for artistic fiction.

In *Dynamic Venus*, the main profile of the story of *Don Alvaro* is embroidered upon by digressions on the nature of love, and by subsidiary plot material. The hero's name now is Gustavo Adolfo Vadillo, and he shares with his namesake—the poet Bécquer—a fine sensibility and appreciation of beauty. Contrary to the outcome of *Don Alvaro*, Adolfo and Isabel do not marry. Instead, each marries another. They meet in Madrid, five years after their first affair, and begin their relationship over again.

Isabel keeps Adolfo waiting in a café for one of their dates; while he waits he reads a novel entitled *La verdad en el pozo*, the plot of which is the same as the plot of "Folletín," part three of the author's *Summer Salon*. Isabel and Adolfo's affair leads to the bedroom where he describes his pleasure in contemplating her beauty. After a bubble bath, Isabel dances naked for Adolfo to the sounds of Falla's "Ritual Dance" on the phonograph next door. Adolfo is so taken by her beauty that he renames her Helen. That night, after attending a concert of music by Hindemith, Adolfo returns home to his wife, to find the pace of life in the country after his exciting encounter with Isabel-Helen very pallid indeed. The epilogue informs us that Adolfo returned to the city to meet Isabel-Helen often.

In this novel are to be found a number of characteristics which we can consider typical of Jarnés' work in the genre. First, there is the incorporation of stories and novelistic material written previously. Second, there are many digressions and long conversations on art, the role of the artist, and the purpose of art in society. Thirdly, we find the beautiful and intelligent heroine whose charm unfailingly impresses and seduces the hero. And lastly, we find the hero disinclined to involve himself in amorous affairs. We share, however, the opinion of Carlos Martínez who, after asking how Jarnés could have written a novel of such frothy inconsequence after the tremendous crisis of the Civil War, remarks: "The least negative thing which, in my opinion, we can say of *La* [*sic*] *Venus dinámica*, is that its appearance was inopportune."[35]

What is apparent is that Jarnés' novelistic vein had been worked out. Perhaps as early as 1932, with *The Red and the Blue*, his capacity for originality in the novel had begun to diminish. We recall that this novel, and the one which preceded it by a year, *Scenes on the Brink of Death*, were continuations respectively of *The Useless Professor* and *The Paper Guest*, the author's first two novels and the ones which confirmed him in his literary career. After 1932, his literary output consisted increasingly of essays, biographies, and translations. We have pointed to some of the more notable instances where Jarnés incorporated into his novels with little significant change material he had previously written; but for limitations of space, we could show this to have been a typical practise whose frequency tended to increase after 1930. Jarnés, furthermore, was unfortunate in that he came to literature late; he was thirty-six when *Father Pedro* was published. When the convulsive events of the Civil War occurred, he was forty-eight, a man of settled literary habits and a fully mature outlook on life.

His inability or disinclination to turn full about in his artistic credo is the source of a large part of the criticism of his work; coming as it usually does from those whose artistic methods have been diametrically opposed to his, or who were still formulating their novelistic positions at the height of the political and social turmoil of the 1930's, we can view it as biased if not also inspired by political animosity.

But despite the bias in such criticisms of Jarnés, there is still the fact that for Spanish writers of the 1930's and 1940's particularly, Jarnés' work has had little meaning or influence. Perhaps an explanation of this fact lies in Jarnés' declining inventiveness in the 1930's. The lesser originality of his work after that time implies that a certain intensity had gone out of his vision and approach to the world about him. He no longer discovered so many "brand-new types of beauty"; his writing no longer conveyed the intense degree of enthusiasm it once had. Perhaps we could say that he had chosen to remain faithful to his literary method of the 1920's rather than to allow that method to change and develop to embrace the world of the 1930's. Guillermo de Torre has written that "whoever writes with truth and intensity about his own present will always be a writer of the present for other ages. On the contrary, whoever begins to be out of date, an anachronism in his own age, will also be out of date for those who come after him. Even if aesthetics change, problems continue across the ages . . ."[36]

Jarnés had begun to lose his actuality in the 1930's, not so much because his literary output had refused to become politically committed, but because it had ceased to convey the same degree of intensity as it had in the preceding decade.

CHAPTER 4

Thematics and Style

I *The Spanish Situation*

A S we have seen, a commonplace criticism of Jarnés' novels
has been that they were detached from the realities of
Spanish life, indifferent to Spain's social and political problems,
in fact, given over to the creation and perpetuation of an "uncommitted" literature. Surely, as far as the novels are concerned,
we do not find the majority to have been focussed on the burning social and political issues of his day. We find no systematic
appraisals of any of the pressing problems which aroused such
heated argument in the 1930's and which politicized all of
Spanish life. In the politicization of literary questions is to be
found much of the motive for the rancor directed at Jarnés by his
critics. It is as if he had defected to the other side, or at least
been remiss in meeting his responsibilities by not himself giving
political substance to his writings.

In the sections which follow, we shall examine in some detail
the extent to which such criticisms of Jarnés are valid. We do
not pretend either to vindicate some claim for his unremitting
liberalism in politics, nor to show him as an intensely political
writer hidden beneath a cloak of artistic metaphor. Rather we
hope to bring some needed attention to those areas of his work
where Jarnés can clearly be seen to take a stand on important
non-literary issues. We have no stake in rehabilitating Jarnés in
literary history. We merely wish to contribute something which
has been lacking in Jarnesian criticism to date, so that others
may perhaps have a wider base upon which to develop a critique
of his works and an estimation of his contribution to the novel.

Jarnés held a view of Spain which was directly in line with that
of his fellow disciples of Ortega. He neither wished to excise the

venerable historical tradition, nor to obliterate Spain's picturesque present reality. On the other hand, neither did he hope to exalt these aspects over what was valuable in Spain's evolving modernity. In 1929, he wrote: "Spain is something more than a handful of Avilas and Toledos, although venerable enough because of them. Spain is something more than a handful of books of mysticism, tales of rascality, and memoirs of adventurers. Spain is a bundle of energies which in large part have not come to light. . . . Here the foreigner has more, much more to see than ruined castles and crowds of ghosts, ghosts who mutter the dubious glories of our useless Cid. Here the foreigner has something more to see and to feel, from the highways to the laboratories."[1]

His disdain for the ghosts who mutter the Cid's glories is not an unqualified one; he would muffle them only to allow the sounds of modern life, traffic, factories, the air hammer, to be heard as well. Jarnés would silence the ghosts only when they seemed to be speaking for the partisans of an outworn myth of Spanish grandeur, a myth as dangerous because of its irrationality as it is incapable of producing anything useful for modern Spain.

Although Jarnés readily acknowledged the part myth plays in the formation of national consciousness,[2] he insisted that myth be kept in its historical place and that it not become an object of contemporary adoration.[3] Since myths are fundamentally irrational, they are often seen as embodiments of man's instinctual urges. Jarnés places restraints on the function of myth in modern life partly because myth, unchecked, may assume disproportionate importance, crowding out what is modern and alive, and partly because of his belief that man's instinctual nature needed to be restrained.

He thought, for example, that much of the political turmoil of the present century was due to the unrestrained expression given, individually in Anarchism and collectively in Communism, to the instincts.[4] We should point out his strictures on myth were meant for myth in public life; myth was allowed to function freely in his literature. Since literature is not life, but a life which cannot totally be lived,[5] myths were admitted frequently into his literary works, where they provide a shorthand for the author's characterizations.

Jarnés' antipathy to the unrestrained expression of the instincts is, in fact, one of the cornerstones of his artistic edifice. He makes of it the basis upon which the imagination and humor (*gracia*) weave an intricate dance. "Grace presupposes law, as the vault presupposes the arch, and reprieve, a code. Laws, laws in order to live! And to live—which in society means to live with—is to obey two kinds of laws: intimate and external. Here is the root of real human freedom. Familial ties, friendship, the necessary civic obligations. Loyalty for one's own, keep intact the law of all for all" (*Euphrosyne or Grace*, p. 39). Jarnés was no libertarian; nor, obviously, was he a rigid traditionalist. Rather he sought to strike a balance between the delightful spontaneity of grace and humor—the joy of discovery of a child—and the graver responsibilities every man had as a member of society. Perhaps it is in observing Jarnés in the act of trying to achieve this balance that we see him falter and, much like a tightrope walker, appear to be producing "acrobatics."

There is a troublesome lack of precision in Jarnés' notions concerning "instincts" and their increasing pressure upon the established order of modern Spanish life. Undoubtedly, one of the primary connotations of the term "instincts" for Jarnés was that of the sexual instincts which, because of the work of Freud and other depth psychologists had come to be the center of much scientific research and discussion in European and American cultural circles in the 1920's and 1930's. Though he nowhere spelled them out, we can infer other connotations which our author saw in the term "instincts"; they were things which we most likely would today call social necessities, or demands for social justice.

It is clear that Jarnés was not proposing to suppress, for example, the demands of the Asturian miners for better working conditions; however, he felt very uncomfortable with the vehemence of the miners' presentation of their demands, and with the violence and destruction which resulted from their confrontations with the police. Perhaps because he was in sympathy with the justice of their demands, he felt their force all the more, and considered them to be as strong as other "instincts" of men.

Another circumstance which should not be ignored in our estimation of Jarnés' notions of the "instincts" is the fundamentalization of political life in the 1930's, exemplified best in the appeal

of Hitler to the "instincts" of the German people. Where the
Spanish experience of the nineteenth century, though surely not
devoid of civil wars and "instinctual" claims from various quarters, had appeared to Jarnés as a fairly ordered although perhaps,
frivolous series of exchanges of power by the political parties,
the claims presented on one or another "instinctual" basis by
parties all across the political spectrum in the Spain of the
1930's must surely have appeared to him as disorganized and
even senseless.

Where labor clamored for the satisfaction of its demands,
capital argued with the persuasion of armed force for the maintenance of order and for the due deliberation of the merit of the
claims. Where the layman urged the specularization of Spanish
life, the orthodox replied with "instinctual" appeals to Spain's
ancient Catholic tradition. Jarnés, the moderate, was more per-
plexed by the violence and seeming irrationality of the claimants
of social and political justice; he sided, we must conclude, with
the orderly processes of established institutions. Had they worked
well in Spain, we might today view him as a temperate man of
liberal persuasions. Since they did not, we cannot but see Jarnés'
moderation—as do so many of his critics—as the response of a
man out of touch with the pressing needs of the disadvantaged
in Spain. It is not historical hindsight alone which leads us to
this conclusion; it is the fact that where polar extremes are in
contention, the response of the moderate represents an inadequate
commitment to the resolution of the extremes.

We ought not to forget, nonetheless, that Jarnés' moderate
theoretical position did not lead him to side with Franco during
the war; indeed, when it came to taking action, he chose to serve
in the Republican Army. But the conflict between what he believed in theory and what he felt impelled to act upon must
have been at the root of much of the depression he felt during
the war.[6]

In addition, we should not overlook a certain element of
aboulia in Jarnés' heroes and, we may legitimately infer, in the
author himself. While perhaps not completely the captives of
the debilitating *mal du siècle* which afflicted certain heroes of
the novels of the Generation of 1898, his male heroes uniformly
shrink from assuming a role which might even remotely be
termed "heroic." They ride no white chargers to the rescue of

maidens; they champion no social or political causes. Since our author's novels do not treat situations systematically, and do not explore the development of his characters across time, it is not surprising that they also lack any comprehensive philosophical rationale for the heroes' aboulia. And, though the heroes are heroes only reluctantly, they do exhibit some slight force of will particularly in the pursuit of beauty, female and artistic. But the force of their will is so attentuated that when they meet with rebuff, their personalities are not shattered.

When it came to evaluating the political events of his time, Jarnés was certainly not a detached observer. He sounded, in 1942, a cry of alarm of the sort which later was to become almost universal, pointing out the dangers for humanity in the advanced technology of destruction which man had developed.[7] In more specific detail, he provides in *Scenes on the Brink of Death,* a portrait of the futility in the actions of both Anarchists and capitalists. For if "the anarchist, who is preparing his bomb to kill two unfortunate soldiers in the royal guard the next day" is a pathetic figure, so is the factory owner "who is inspecting the night shift in a factory which, before a month is up, will be invaded by communism" (p. 12). He sides neither with the one nor the other.

If we were to situate Jarnés on the political scale, we should probably do so to the left of center. His anti-clerical feelings, which we will examine below, his dislike of dictatorships left or right, his sympathies for his fellow man, all support such a position. His disdain for an unruly proletariat stems from an antipathy to the proletariat *per se.*

Yet, he was never doctrinaire politically; and if he aspired to a newer and more just social order, he thought that that order lay in the future.[8] To the extent that Jarnés' aspirations for a better social order in Spain lay in the distant future we can term him a dreamer or a visionary. Thus, Jarnés would merit the sympathy he himself directed to other dreamers, for example Francisco Ferrer (*The Red and the Blue,* p. 116).

By classifying Jarnés with the visionaries, we seek merely to point out his general disdain, especially before 1936, for direct militant political action. Of course, when the Civil War broke out he, along with many other writers and intellectuals, served the immediate needs of the Republic through active service in the army. Except for the years of the Civil War, he took no direct political action. Not only was he himself not a politician; in addition, he had rather more respect for the orderly flow of political events than to permit himself to join one group or another in the production of strident political claims. He strongly stigmatized such discordant and vociferous outcries as a rupture of a law of harmony, even while recognizing that the situation was very much a part of his era (*The Red and the Blue*, pp. 173-74).

Yet another reason for Jarnés' abstention from overt political activity was his belief that political ideas, when they become solidified into doctrine, are as sterile as the countless "isms" which abounded in the field of art. Attacking the Anarchists in particular, he wrote: "The anarchist's ideas are barely cells of ideas. They prefer them to be free of all concreteness, devitalized; they're of no use" (*Paula and Paulette*, p. 174). We see here our author's opposition to definitions and abstractions which, devoid of any living content, tend to stultify rather than to invigorate thought. Also, we have another glimpse of his antipathy to whatever was anti-vital; we may again gauge the distance between Jarnés and "dehumanization" of which he was never a partisan.

Jarnés saw the contradiction inherent in a writer's espousing a political cause. For while a political partisan cannot espouse or be in agreement with that portion of the truth which favors his enemy, "a writer must not ignore [it]. Therefore, if he is truly a writer he will end up by attracting the enmity of those in his own camp. The fate of every writer faithful to his conscience is to be crucified. The politician doesn't tolerate truth; he only tolerates slogans" (quoted by Ontañón, *Viaje y aventura de los escritores de España*, p. 193). The validity of this opinion has become increasingly apparent in the years since the end of World War II when a great many writers have recanted of their previous political partisanship.[9]

The attacks on Jarnés for not producing a "committed" literature often come from a sector which wants literature to be subordinated to life. Jarnés did believe that literature should use life as its stimulus; he simply refused to restrict "life" to political events or the current social issues.[10] He had written "We need chroniclers who can put our Age clearly so that future genera-

tions will understand and admire us" (*Vivien and Merlin*, p. 142).
He saw the "committed" writers as too often aspirants to political
power; what they wrote was therefore suspect because of their
ulterior motives. He also saw them as partisans of the instinctual
and impulsive claims which they depicted in their works. "Let
us distrust men who, in any land, 'prefer' nudity. Let us distrust
politicians, writers, all those who prefer to adhere to the 'history
of the will,' to return to the instinctual, to the spontaneous, to
the sincere . . . and other inaccessible marvels. Isn't that the best
way to escape cold—and ironic—reason? That is the history of
contemporary cynicism" (*Escuela de libertad* [*School for Freedom*], p. 11).

Jarnés felt it imperative to continue producing works which
might give later generations a picture of his own. For only by
doing so could the spiritual history of Spain be continued. The
spiritual history was always separate from Spain's political history; although at times they might parallel each other, the
former was never subordinated to the latter (*Ariel dispero* [*Ariel
in Flight*], p. 250). Thus in his way—to be sure, not in the way his
critics would have preferred—Jarnés was committed to depicting
present-day Spain.

As much as he believed in the value of what was vital in
Spanish life, Jarnés also thought that the vital must be tempered
or restrained by reason. He characterized the nineteenth century
in Spain as an age without reason; passion it had, vehemence and
splendid temperaments, but no capacity for meditation or reflection (*Sor Patrocinio* [*Sister Patrocinius*], p. 13). In political
movements such as Carlism, which confused political with religious ardor (*ibid.*, p. 62), Jarnés saw primarily a lamentable lack
of judgment. Reason is sharpened by asking questions, but tradition and dogma are founded in faith.

Always upholding the value of reason, Jarnés attacked the
exaggerations of dogma and traditionalism.[11] For example, coun-
tering those who believed that a special favor was conferred on
Spain by dint of her having colonized the New World, of her
having been "the cradle of the race," he wrote: "But in our
language of today—as truthful as it is aseptic—a cradle is, simply,
a way station—the first—on the twisting highway of life" (*Cartas
al Ebro* [*Letters to the Ebro*], p. 131). Of course, Jarnés implies
here that what is most important is what is happening now, not

what happened in the past; we shall rise or fall on the basis of how we confront the things which lie ahead of us on life's highway, not on the basis of any special merit conferred on us by illustrious forebears. These ideas are certainly action-oriented and forward-looking. They help us to understand our author as one of a generation in Spain which was breaking new ground in many areas of cultural, political, and social life.

Jarnés knew that granting a preeminent position to Spain's past would turn the nation into a "gilded mummy" (*Letters to the Ebro*, p. 168). But it had graver dangers than that, for it might allow the revival of dangerous and even deadly institutions long extinct. Jarnés criticized the film *Don Quixote* because he thought it tried to portray not so much seventeenth-cenutry Spain as "eternal Spain": "The very Spain of today, which lacks very little for a return to the burning of enlightened books" (*Cita de ensueños* [*A Date with Illusion*], p. 107). Written in 1936, these comments show a clear concern with political reality. And even earlier, in 1928, he had cast his lot with the modern age, calling the Middle Ages a "noble old woman" who deserved to be locked up in a museum (*The Paper Guest*, pp. 72-73). Like Costa, who called for the Cid's chest to be locked up with seven keys, Jarnés puts history behind him and concerns himself with the present.

Perhaps this attitude is one of the reasons why the characters in his novels show little or no development over the course of a given book. In order to do so, they would have to have a past, a history, which the author and reader both would take in the manner of an explanation of their conduct in the novel. But if Jarnés devalued the past, his own as well as his country's, how could he believe a character's past to be an ingredient essential for the novel's comprehension?

Additionally, postulating causative factors in a character's background would open a Pandora's box allowing all sorts of irrational and fortuitous events to spring forth. By their nature, these events would be beyond authorial control, intractable to the author's reason. How much simpler it is to provide the character with no past or with a past which he disavows or ignores, and to set him off in the direction of future adventures. Then his destiny can be controlled with the author's sole obligation that of respecting his character's memory of events he has already experienced in the novel.

Further, we should remember that endowing a character with a personal history means involving him in the social milieu of family, class, and community which gave him his origin. For Jarnés, who wished to attend principally to one character at a time—hence the sketchiness and underdevelopment of his secondary characters—the depiction of a hero's social milieu might mute his individuality, might make him blend into a more or less amorphous or complex group. Jarnés was not so naive as to think that the social milieu played no part in influencing the character; he was simply more interested in what the character did than in how he came to do it. In a musical analogy he said that the "social orchestra" should be considered the background for the solo performances of talented individuals (*The Red and the Blue*, p. 175).

II *Anticlericalism*

Criticism of the Church, the clergy, and of religion generally has had a time-honored place in Spanish literature since at least the sixteenth century. From the *Lazarillo de Tormes* on, there have been few aspects of Spanish Catholicism which have escaped criticism.[12] In a country renowned as "more Papist than the Pope," we should not expect the contrary opinion to have gone unexpressed. With regard to Jarnés, who himself had at one time contemplated a clerical career but then turned away from it, we shall try to show the scope of his criticism as well as its tone.

While the criticism is harsh and direct, it does not pretend to either a reformation of the Church or its disestablishment. Jarnés considered that the nature of the Church as he knew it was not susceptible of reform. Further, it would have been a violation of its own nature if the Church were abruptly to reform itself. Rather our author's comments are expository, perhaps in some measure explanatory of his own separation from the Church, but not designed to reform.

Nor did the question of disestablishment, which so concerned some of his contemporaries, seem to have preoccupied him. We would suggest that such a matter, because of its legal and governmental intricacies, lay outside the area of Jarnés' self-defined competence. In fact, as we have mentioned previously, Jarnés almost never addressed himself to specific governmental problems, and when he did he never prescribed alternatives for action.

It is not uncommon to find in discussions of literary anticlericalism some statement to the effect that the writer in question, whatever his criticisms of churchly abuses, still remained a Catholic, or that he did not leave the Catholic religion. Such statements are often designed to preserve a semblance of orthodoxy in judgments of the religious, as if to show that beneath the criticism of the abuses of a particular priest or a particular activity of the Church there lay in the writer a fundamental faith unshaken. As far as we have been able to discover, such was not the case with Jarnés. Having left the seminary, he seems to have left the Catholic religion and his religious faith behind him. Nowhere in his works after 1928, so far as we know, does Catholicism appear in a favorable light. Where he turned his attention to religious figures, as in *Sister Patrocinius*, he was apt to see the individual's accomplishments as having been gained without religious inspiration, perhaps even in spite of his religion.

The most fundamental fault Jarnés found with Catholicism was its authoritarianism. Particularly in convent or monastery life, he found rigidified ritual and strict authority to be stultifying. He called the nineteenth-century nun, Sor Patrocinio, the result of four hundred years of "fanatical ignorance, of desires to conquer, of unthinking although astute, thirst for power" (*Sister Patrocinius*, p. 15). As Jarnés saw it, the petrification of ritual over the course of twenty centuries had left no unanswered questions, no room for debate (*Paula and Paulette*, p. 131). In his disdain for doctrinal rigidities in any field, and out of his love for what was alive and changeable, he criticized the clergy for giving its attention to general and abstract problems, rather than to "the beauties of any human group in the flesh" (*The Red and the Blue*, p. 185).

Seminary life, designed to produce experts in ritual and Church doctrine, was devoid of "any grace [*gracia*], of any vital rhythm" (*The Paper Guest*, p. 54). The conclusion Jarnés drew was that ritual was what remained of religions "when the substance had been squeezed out" (*Vivien and Merlin*, p. 129).

Jarnés thought the mercenary Church particularly worthy of contempt. He scorned the medieval Church for trading on the fears of the faithful that the world might end after the first millenium, issuing in return for a "splendid donation" its signature on an "I.O.U. payable in another, more reliable world."[13] He accused the Church of capitalizing on the fear of Hell, of fostering it, in order to "sell indulgences, like trout" (*Paula and Paulette*, p. 164). The Church coveted more than money and power; it coveted the souls of the unconverted. Jarnés likened African missionaries to slave traders; the traders kidnapped natives while the missionaries kidnapped souls.[14] The result is that the priest is dressed in a housecoat of merino wool, and a peasant in trousers and jacket of corduroy . . ." (*The Red and the Blue*, pp. 14-15). The fact that the novel just cited presents a condensation of Marxist political thinking does not detract from the force of Jarnés' position.

Jarnés' biography of Sor Patrocinio provides an excellent example in detail and at length of the attitudes we are examining.[15] Sor Patrocinio, having refused to marry the man her family selected for her, entered the order of the Immaculate Conception of Our Lady, taking her final vows in 1830, three months before her nineteenth birthday, and after many visitations from heaven and from the foundress of the Order.

Our biographer cuts through the welter of pious tradition surrounding Sor Patrocinio—her visitations, her stigmata—to reveal her true motives in taking charge of the convent at Torrelaguna; rather than on the religious fervor of a foundress, these were based on her will to power (*ibid.*, pp. 133-34). She became in the cloister an example of an emerging political class in Spain, the *cacique* or political boss (*ibid.*, p. 135). Jarnés documents the nun's access to the royal purse strings (*ibid.*, p. 151), and with great irony presents her setbacks at the hands of the anticlerical laity from her own point of view: "The new barbarians of the nineteenth century open graves, scatter skeletons . . ." (*ibid.*, p. 181). In a tone very much like Larra's, Jarnés stresses the lamentable conditions which prevailed in Spain among laity and clergy alike. "Rumor—that harebrained son of Ignorance—is now striking its last blind blows. (We personify these beings because in this attempt at biography they are the main characters: Rumor, with its eyes blindfolded, and Ignorance, with its eyes wide open, but staring vacantly)" (*ibid.*, p. 216).

Perhaps the best means by which the Church maintained its

position was by keeping the faithful in ignorance. Jarnés sarcastically noted that the absence of heresy in León in the tenth century was due to the general ignorance of the population, "the enviable state of the true believers."[16] Nothing could seem more reprehensible to a writer of Jarnés' intellectual bent. But the ignorance fostered by the clergy did not confine itself to intellectual matters alone; it embraced the entire world. In 1932, Jarnés depicts a young boy who "knows no way to conquer this visible world because they only taught him the ways to conquer the invisible one" (*The Red and the Blue*, p. 16).

In what might seem an elaborate sort of punning, Jarnés was often given to pointing out contradictions in Catholicism, some innocuous, some quite serious. He remarked on the pleasure the historian finds in discovering that Jesus numbered among his ancestors prostitutes and murderers.[17] Or he took a serio-comic interest in young Julio's confused perceptions of female pulchritude; the breast of the girls of the town are equated in his perceptions with the heavenly breast of "Mary of Nazareth, seated on a wooden cloud of blue and silver, in the center of the great altarpiece of the church" (*The Paper Guest*, p. 31).

On a more serious plane, he strongly criticized the Church's involvement in worldly, particularly political, matters. In Spain, for example, he saw a large part of the nation's history, "the unpublished, that is, the real" history, as involved with the Church's domination of political affairs (*Sister Patrocinius*, p. 43). In 1933, he was commenting on "the religious terrain, the political terrain, and the mixed terrain, of which we in Spain still have innumerable hectares" (*Fauna contemporánea* [*Contemporary Animal Life*], p. 25). Jarnés was directly in the mainstream of the liberal thinking of his day in condemning the established Church for its political involvement. His anticlericalism, however, remained always reasoned rather than impassioned. We do not know the extent to which he may have felt animosity due to the Church's unfortunate influence on his own early life.

He seems not to have borne any life-long grudge; nor was he to feel so intimately affected by the Church as to be unable, as was apparently James Joyce, to surmount his antipathy toward it. For after 1936, the anticlerical vein in his writing is diminished. Perhaps leaving Spain for exile in a Mexico which had already achieved the sort of *détente* sought by the Second Republic relieved the pressing nature of the problem for him.

III   *Grace, Wit, and Happiness*

This theme is one which is as prevalent in our author's works as the two which we have just examined. Consideration of it will help us better to understand Jarnés' position on certain central artistic problems and permit us to evaluate some of his novelistic strengths and weaknesses. The theme was never far from his mind, and we find mention of it in his early novels. *The Paper Guest* and *Paula and Paulette,* throughout his later career to *Euphrosyne or Grace* and the three anthologies of humorous anecdotes that he edited in Mexico, *La sal del mundo (The Spice of Life), El sueño de las calaveras (The Playboys' Dream)* and *La taberna por vecina (The Neighborhood Tavern).*

Brook, the main character of the second section of *Paula and Paulette* says that "the most profound art on Earth is the art of laughter" (p. 205). In addition, it is an art which never gained much sway among common people who are "so disposed to let themselves be contaminated by crying" (*ibid.,* p. 207). Our first glimpse at the theme shows a certain aversion in Jarnés to the common people, and a claim of nobility or aristocracy for laughter. We shall see this claim repeated quite often. The main objective of wit *(la gracia)* is to make everything it touches pleasant. "Therefore, wit is a social value, since it serves as a subtle bond between the witty *(el agraciado)* and others. Thus, a work of art, achieved in wit *(en gracia)* or with wit, ought above all to set up sympathetic currents between the author and spectator . . ."[18] We should notice here the multiple meanings of which Jarnés makes use. The phrase *en gracia* naturally has predominantly religious connotations; its use here confers on the artist who is witty, who has "grace," an almost divine favor. As we shall see, this notion is not quite the same as the Romantic one which held that the artist, *because* he was an artist, was divinely inspired. For wit or grace is not something which automatically belongs to an artist; it comes only through careful cultivation, and only to the mature.

Adolfo, in *The Paper Guest,* says that he could neither hate nor smile—he was too young (p. 137). The ability to smile is given only to older people who have managed to forget the unhappiness of their past. For happiness *(la alegría)* is "the product of a final victory over the formless, the rude materials offered up by instinct, events, 'volcanic' passion . . ." *(Paula and Paulette,* p. 207). The mark of the author's own unhappy past can be seen in these comments. It would seem that one of the main sources of happiness in our author's life was his successful resistence of "instincts"; what these might have been we cannot say, because of the lack of adequate biographical material. However, in its general outlines, this is essentially an obedient posture. That is, since the instincts are identified with the id—and, as the author so often remarked, with the turbid nether regions of the unconscious—the successful resistance of the demands of the instincts constitutes a victory for the superego, for the assimilated forces of order and authority within the author.

This fundamentally obedient stance helps explain why Jarnés' writings on avant-garde theories of the novel, or his reviews of other authors, lack a combative or highly rebellious tone. He propounded his theory of the novel with a measured calm and without virulent attacks upon his predecessors or contemporaries. Aside from considerations of professional modesty, or authorial humility, the absence of a marked iconoclastic tone is due to his stand against rebelliousness because it was a sign of unrestrained impulses.

The matter may be viewed in another light as well. As we saw above (p. 107 ff.), Jarnés conceived of the instincts as rebellious demands for action. He evidently felt the demands to be so rigorous that he saw the resistance to them as a heroic act. In a maneuver of spiritual economy, he balanced the demands against the resistance, and was able to derive the satisfactions of heroism from winning the battle against the demands. It is clear to us that the demands must be thought to stem from the instincts, since these are inherent, not readily controllable, and most important, not subject to modification by the action of will. If the demands had been thought to stem from desires or wishes, they would then be volitional and subject to modification and control by the will. But if, as we suspect, the author suffered from a reduced force of will, if he undervalued efforts of the will, then he could hardly hope to do battle successfully with his desires. Viewing the demands as instinctual helped rationalize his losses in such battles, as well as confer on him a hero's stature when he won them.

Unhappiness, in our author's opinion, was essentially unproductive; Jarnés did not think we could profit much from our unfortunate and sad experiences. While it was difficult to forget past unhappiness, the ability to do so was the mark of creativity *(el ingenio);* few people will thank the one who "at the risk of seeming superficial, refuses to plunge into the mire of trivial psychology, terrain marked out by science."[19] The natural climate of creativity is happiness, and we should do all we can to make creativity accessible to everyone: "Let us—I repeat—bring the great spirits down from their pedestals, so the good public may be familiar with them" *(The Spice of Life,* p. 24).

Here we see Jarnés' affirmation of his mission as a spreader of culture. Quite in keeping with ideals common to his generation—to Ortega and the *Revista de Occidente* in particular—Jarnés saw himself as the purveyor of the great works of European and World culture to the Spain of his day. This does not imply popularization or debasement, but rather facilitating the Spaniard's acquisition of a wider culture through translations, literary reviews and, equally important, by showing him that the common denominator of creative genius everywhere was its joy *(alegría),* its ability to create happiness in the reader. "The creative [*lo ingenioso*] is not superficial. If it were, it would lose its qualities of subtlety and descend to the humble condition of the jest, the joke, the funny saying" *(Letters to the Ebro,* p. 35).

One of the things humor *(la gracia)* carries with it is a profound sense of comfort for Jarnés. In the words of one of his heroes, he calls it his last resort *(The Paper Guest,* p. 114). Humor and joy are the products not only of maturity but also of a balanced mind: Proust and Nietzsche, both ill, had "the marvelous joy [*alegría*] which is only born out of a prodigious mental balance" *(The Spice of Life,* p. 20). We may safely infer that Jarnés' notions of joy which we are examining here are related—as he assumed them to be in Proust and Nietzsche—to the maintenance of his spiritual balance in the midst of his own illness.

The question of balance, itself of fundamental importance in Jarnés' work, is seen in another passage written in 1928: "Joy [*júbilo*] and sadness are the same thing for art. So long as sadness does not sink into the disturbed lake of the sentiments and joy contains its confusion so as not to fall into equally disturbed intoxication" *(Ariel in Flight,* p. 41). We note here a tone of sobriety in the midst of joy, of restraint in the face of emotional extremes. Although he never specifies it as such, Jarnés' attitude invokes a sort of Golden Mean in which reason holds the feelings in check.

Our author sought to combine reason and emotion in a carefully balanced equation. "Enthusiasm in effect, is not a good friend of technique, just as the *homo romanticus* [Romantic man] is no friend of *homo faber* [man-the-maker]; but, in this dispute, I decide always to vote for a third, for the *romanticus faber* [the Romantic maker], for vigilant vehemence. This is not eclecticism; it is integralism, to give it some name" (*Sobre la gracia artística* [*On Artistic Grace*] pp. 15-16). In these years, 1931-32, Jarnés was elaborating further notions of "integralism" as we saw in his *Theory of the Top-String.* He hoped to harmonize factions usually at war in man without giving undue weight either to his spiritual, earthly (practical), or emotional needs. Although he never spelled out the technique by which this fusion could be effected in literature, its importance is attested to by its frequent recurrence in his work. He borrowed the passage just quoted for *Euphrosyne or Grace,* written six years after the lecture *On Artistic Grace,* but not published until 1948. In *Euphrosyne* he amplifies on the passage by warning against indulgence in Romantic ecstasies or, even worse, visits to the "sewers of the unconscious filthied by pathology, in subterranean mud"; he asks, "Why not, in art, come to count on the three planes, the underground, *terra firma,* the vague and luminous blue?" (pp. 140-41).

Again, we miss any concrete suggestions as to how the three planes might be harmonized. In fact, because they suggestively parallel Freud's triparte division of id, ego and superego, we are tempted to view Jarnés' "integralism" as a variety of what the psychologists would call the "integrated personality." Yet, because of our author's antipathy to the unconscious, to which he usually refers as a sort of muddy or filthy sewer, and to man's spiritual side, which he saw as a part of man's religious nature and hence tended to undervalue, we cannot perceive the balance he is seeking. For surely if the spiritual-religious and the unconscious are devalued, then the earthly side of man, his reason triumphant, is the primary factor in the *romanticus faber*.

In fact, there is a nice correspondence between Jarnés' "integralism" and his method of fictional characterization. The author's "integralism" gives lesser weight to the unconscious (i.e., the id impulses), and to the spiritual-religious (i.e., the superego), than to the earthly side of man (i.e., the ego). Symbolically, Jarnés is undervaluing respectively the past and the future of the individual; for just as the id represents man's "instincts" and thus is the basic starting point in each individual's life, the superego represents the ideals the individual strives for, hence is a measure of what he hopes to achieve in the future. Likewise, as we have already seen, Jarnés' characters are concentrated in fictional terms in their own present-time activties. We may learn a little about their pasts, and a bit about their futures (what happened to them after the novel's action ceased). But their importance hinges on what they do in the present.

For this reason, so many of his characters are willing to accept new adventures as they present themselves. Since the characters are not functioning as ambitious projections into the future, since they are not particularly concerned with "becoming" anything, the acceptance of a new adventure does not disrupt their plans, or interfere with any trajectory they have previously mapped out for themselves. Likewise, when a character is primarily depicted in the present moment, when his past and future are relatively ignored by the author, there is little point in the author's showing us the links in the character between what he is now and what he was or will be. Hence, there is no point in attending to the development of the character from what he was into what he will be.

Now, if a character is presented primarily in his present-time activities, and cut adrift both from his past and his future, his novelistic conduct tends to consist of actions or episodes all located in more or less the same time period; i.e., his experiences are all concentrated in a short time span, and are assimilated by him without any particular one having a decisive effect on his character. There are no "turning points" in the careers of Jarnés' characters; no bursting insights at mid-novel which make them change their direction. And, since the characters' experiences are episodic, and all approximately equal in their importance for them, they might all as well have been presented in a different sequence, and their number might be added to or subtracted from without greatly altering the portraiture.

Beyond this difficulty, the absence of a clear notion of how to harmonize man's three aspects, lies another. Jarnés nowhere spells out his ideas of how the three aspects of man are related chronologically. He does not say how these aspects were to be harmonized in the act of writing. In *Euphrosyne or Grace,* he briefly refers to Emerson's ideas on intelligence, saying that the "healthy writer" goes through a series of "expansions and contractions," taking flight away from Earth, turning inward to consider his gifts, and touching Earth to receive new inspiration (pp. 43-44). But this sheds no light on the act of writing, for in this the critical matter is the role of memory. Granted that the writer's vehemence may be restrained by a vigilant intelligence. But it is the intelligence, acting as the writer's inner censor, which must pass judgment on the memories which remain from the experiences the writer has when he is not writing. And it is here that we come to an obstacle difficult to surmount, for Jarnés tended to deny his memories entrance into his works. We need but recall his hostility toward autobiography (in "Años de aprendizaje y alegría," p. 18), and his frequent refusals to write about his own past to see that memory is devalued as a productive source of the writer's inspiration. We do not mean to imply, of course, that all writing must be autobiographical; we do not yet understand well enough the ways an author's creativity or imagination transforms his memories. We mean merely to point to a confusion in what otherwise appears a reasonable and even practical prescription.

If, as it seems, the writer's creativity goes hand-in-hand with his happiness, his happiness is a quality of temperament and not "a reward for long suffering, or the expression of a vice: a concept fostered among the people by the lives of the saints and serialized novels" (*The Paper Guest,* p. 29). The artist's happiness also confers on him a special rank denied the common man; what the mass of people can never forgive the genius is his happiness "because it is precisely his happiness—his rotund affirmation of himself—which situates him above other men" (*The Spice of Life,* p. 19).

Jarnés compared laughter with crying and found that the latter deformed men and made them uniformly ugly. However, smiling and laughter tend "to create personal styles, to present original profiles of the spirit. To create, in sum, new beauties" (*Paula and Paulette,* p. 208). Recalling our author's interest in depicting original and new forms of beauty, we can easily see why he favors laughter which he thought produces them. What is not immediately clear is why grief does not produce equally original forms of beauty. No sentimentalist, he could not agree that grief could produce beauty, in his characters or in life. A confirmed optimist, Jarnés built his notions of artistic beauty around mirth and joy. He seems to have rejected—at least for his own writing, the possibility that aesthetic beauty and pleasure could be produced by a theatrical tragedy, for example, or by an elegy. As we shall see shortly when we turn to his remarks on Lorca, his position is not quite clearly formulated.

Euphrosyne or Grace was published after Jarnés' return to Spain, although he had completed it ten years earlier in 1938. It presents in fifteen chapters and an epilogue a series of dialogues between Julio and Eufrosina on the theme of humor and grace. Eufrosina was one of the three Grecian Graces, goddesses of beauty. She had first appeared in Jarnés' works as a character in *Paula and Paulette* in 1929. The lecture Jarnés delivered in Madrid in April, 1932, at the German-Spanish Center for Intellectual Exchange, and which was published the same year with the title *On Artistic Grace,* sets forth some of his ideas on the subject. But in *Euphrosyne* we find a fuller though still not systematic treatment of it.

Jarnés began by restating the social value of humor *(la gracia);* it is valuable because it establishes a dialogue between the author and the reader: "And to cultivate this dialogue is one of our first duties toward our fellows" (p. 3). This does not imply that the writer should write to please his reader; on the contrary, he should adhere to his own inner message, and hope that from it will flow "sparks with which to ignite or, even better, illuminate people" (p. 4). Jarnés saw the dialogue as a means of allowing the reader to contemplate the beauty in what he reads, to enjoy it, and then, withdrawing from the author, to prolong or extend that beauty in himself. Unamuno, on the contrary wished to incite the reader to the acknowledgement in himself of the anguished problems presented in his dialogue with Unamuno. Since Unamuno wished to draw the reader into himself, his view of dialogue is, in a sense, centripetal; Jarnés, content to give off sparks which illuminate and may even be carried away by the reader, holds a centrifugal view.

Slowness—Ortega's *delectatio morosa*—and elegance may produce humor if they are combined carefully (p. 19). But there are no definitions of humor: "We cannot say that it *is* this or that. But we can say that it is *here* or *there*. How unhappy is the one who is funny [*gracioso*]! How happy is the one who is in humor [*en gracia*]! . . . Humor springs, like a flower, from the man in humor, whether he is an artist or not. To try to *make* it is like trying to find the formula for perpetual motion" *(ibid.)*. We begin to see developing the inner core of Jarnés' notions of humor, a core which, we must admit, is irreducible in its quasi-mystical nature. Humor is, simply, hitting the nail on the head; it is spontaneous, but presupposes a hidden drive "and a magic power of arrangement, of arriving at the unexpected by means of a law, whether artistic or vital, earthly or celestial, organic or geometric" (p. 20).

Humor, then, is produced by an artist in a prior mood or state of *gracia* who contravenes some law. An example from *Paula and Paulette* which comes quickly to mind is the hero's mistake in entering Paula's room in the hotel. Following the "law" that numbers all the rooms on the same side of the corridor with either odd or even numbers, the hero calculates which door should be his. But in this case, the law has not been followed by the management, and the rooms are numbered consecutively up one side of the corridor and down the other. Here, as in other examples of "laws" which are evaded, Jarnés seems in agreement with Bergson's assertion that humor arises out of a situation in which man enacts the rigidities of an automaton or machine.

Yet, for Jarnés, it was not the depiction of man in mechanized rigidity which was in itself humorous; it was man breaking out of that rigidity after having been caught up in it. Since he was no proponent of that rigidity and since, in fact, he saw in it deplorable evidence of "dehumanization"—as witness his attitudes towards the regimentation of life in the army and the seminary —he sees humor only when man surmounts the rigidity and, exercising his vital forces, his impulsive vehemence, gains his freedom from it. Jarnés is helped by the double meaning of the word *gracia;* we tend to think that in viewing man asserting his humanity against rigid "laws" Jarnés saw rather more of the man's "grace" than of his "humor."

Here too we can follow Jarnés' notion of the "instincts" to a further development. As we saw above (pp. 106 ff.), happiness resulted from a successful battle against the instincts. Clearly, instincts are a form of rigidity, since a given instinct exists in quest of a given satisfaction and not of some other. The instinctual life of the lower animals follows set, invariant patterns: nest building, migratory and courtship behavior, etc. An element of humor is present, in Jarnés' opinion, when man manages to evade the rigidities demanded by his instinctual life, when he manages to escape the rigidity into an area of free choice, or even of gratuitiousness.

Because of his stress on the ineffable gift the writer must have in order to create *gracia,* Jarnés reminds us of Lorca's essay on the theory of the *duende.* But whereas Lorca's explanation of the special fire and genius of the Flamenco guitarist or dancer is itself partly tongue-in-cheek, Jarnés is quite serious in *Euphrosyne or Grace.*

Jarnés also attributes the ineffable qualities of humor to Spanish folk music and popular lyrics. These have *ángel* which can become contaminated by commercialism, just as can the *ángel* of the writer whose "diabolical and cold aim is to extract some monetary juice from the latest passional event [or] from the political moment . . ." (p. 27). In add'tion to commercialism or literary opportunism, the decline of humor in the culture is the result of "the cult of the instincts, the cult of power" (p. 39). Jarnés criticizes writers of the latter category as adherents of the "picturesque doctrine of willfulness [*caprichismo*]" (p. 44), for they think they need obey no rules in writing. And in a revealing passage he adds: "This spiritual bread which he no doubt needs and goes to find in the book or the newspaper—the good citizen doesn't want to get it from an acrobat [*malabarista*]" (*ibid.*). Jarnés here seems to be recanting somewhat from his adherence to what his critics call "verbal acrobatics"; the "good citizen" makes an appearance—let us not forget that this is written at the height of the Civil War—as a mute reproach to the excessive pyrotechnics of writers in the preceding decade.

Humor, then, the "spice of life" (p. 56), uncontaminated by commericalism, by a thirst for power, or by excesses of verbal style, will regain its place as the source of the smile, the gesture which distinguishes man from other beasts (p. 57). The place which humor will regain is marked by "nobility, purity, freedom, and happiness" (p. 64), all traits of the highest human aspiration. To help humor regain its place, Jarnés proclaims "the essential happiness of man in the fullness of action and passion, of activity and generosity. Also in full control of his impulses and his opinions" (p. 87). Again we see the balanced, moderate position, the restraint of the instincts, and the rule of reason.

In a way, this call to reason, coming as it does in the midst of the fratricidal irrationality of the Civil War, and from a writer whose public career had been forged in the heated exchanges of manifestos between groups in the vanguard of literary irrationality, must strike us as a little outdated and perhaps even sad. It is as if Jarnés, at age fifty, had lost some of the flexibility or permeability which characterized his work in the 1920's. When he declares that the two great powers in the world are "profit, the golden calf, and humor [*la gracia*], its sincere enemy" (p. 106), we are carried back to the turn of the century to writers like Rodó and Martí whose visions of reality often seem equally simplistic. As an assessment of the situation in the 1930's the terms are simply inadequate.

Euphrosyne or Grace offers some lengthy discussions of the humor, magic and artistry in the animated cartoons of Walt Disney.[20] In some scenes with Mickey Mouse, Jarnés saw more original poetic material than in the poems of Rubén Darío, although he faults the cartoons for their persistent jazz quality which is tiresome on occasion (p. 162). Julio and Eufrosina see a production of Lorca's *Yerma*, which Julio implies has grace (p. 189). In the ensuing discussion, Jarnés praises Lorca's *Romancero gitano*, *Bodas de sangre*, and *Yerma* for their theatrical and pictorial qualities (pp. 189-205). He does not mention *La casa de Bernarda Alba*, perhaps because he did not know that play. And he does not attempt to answer the question of whether the plays are tragedies, and therefore incapable of producing aesthetic pleasure. Since Lorca is the only contemporary Spaniard discussed here, and since the discussion seems fairly arbitrary within the book's structure, we see it as a Jarnesian tribute, one among a great many written during the war and after, to the Grenadine poet killed in the first year of the Civil War.

Having become of one mind on the subject of humor and grace, through the dialogues we have just reviewed, Eufrosina and Julio are fused into one being and their story ends. In this attempt to work out his concept of humor and happiness, Jarnés ends on a note which is a symbolic wish: that Euphrosyne, one of the Graces, shall join with him and infuse his work with the ineffable gift of humor, thereby placing him in a state of artistic grace.

We should note the development of Jarnés' ideas on grace and humor, for it shows some of the effects of the changing times on his work. If in the mid-1920's vanguard writers had rediscovered happiness *(la alegría)*,²¹ it was as a function of the humorous side of Dadaism, the reaction to the so serious purposes with which the Generation of 1898 invested literature, and the need for a literary escape valve after the traumatic Great War. The high principles and achievements of art, literary and pictorial, were called into question, and it was fashionable for artists to try to deflate their occupations and reputations with irreverent and nihilistic frivolity.²²

Initially, Jarnés' notions seem of a piece with those of the irreverent Surrealists. In his early novels, particularly in *The Paper Guest,* an additional source of his demand for humor is his need for a corrective to the sombre and highly serious atmosphere of the seminary and the army. But as the decade of the 1930's approached, some of Jarnés' ideas on humor began to change. The antic, Chaplinesque side of humor was toned down, leaving in *Theory of the Top-String* the less pointed humor of a child at play. With his lecture *On Artistic Grace,* we see Jarnés trying to work out a serious justification for humor in literature, endowing it with high purpose and special virtues. By the time he wrote *Euphrosyne or Grace,* he had refined out of his notions any of the hectic and frivolous aspects which remained, and conferred on humor the preeminent role of doing battle with "profit" as a literary motive.

We doubt that this development responds to a motive other than the increasing gravity of the Spanish and European political situation. By 1938, events had moved Jarnés into the enunciation of what we could call a theory of "committed humor" in literature. In addition to upholding the forces of purity, nobility, and disinterest in literature, humor now had to serve as a means of dialogue between author and reader; that is, it had taken on an important social function. To say that Jarnés' writings failed to reflect the social and political events of his day, then, is to overlook the development of this theme and of its value for the author for whom humor had become serious.

IV Style and Structure

For Jarnés, the artist and his style were one and the same.[23] One could not have one without the other. And style meant for our author primarily a distinctive verbal style, rather than unique ways of handling the novel's structure, or unique points of view for the characters. A good deal of the Jarnesian style is based on his preference for concrete and specific words used in new and unexpected contexts. Vagueness of expression indicated to him vagueness of thought (*Exercises*, p. 11). Although not as extreme in his search for *le mot juste* as Flaubert had been, Jarnés insisted on precision in language.

Hence, we find in his work an extensive vocabulary of technical terms from mathematics, painting, technology, commerce, and other fields, as well as a goodly number of neologisms, foreign borrowings, and obsolete or archaic words revived. The artist needed to lay claim to the precise words whatever their origins, and he placed on them no severe demands that they be words enshrined in the Academy's dictionary: "It's good to call things by their names, but it's better to find beautiful names for things" (*Exercises*, p. 38). Just as Jarnés was interested in discovering new forms of beauty *(bellezas inéditas)*, he was apt to consider beautiful a new and original name discovered for something primarily *because* it was new and original. He thought of himself, as countless writers before him had, as an alchemist of language; implicitly, his patron is Dedalus, artificer to the gods. "For each ingot of copper handed me by men and objects, I can return an ingot of gold" (*The Useless Professor*, p. 106). Whether derived from Joyce's Stephen Dedalus or directly from the god of the Greek myth, we can note the poetic stance: the poet transmutes the base metal of everyday life and language into the precious gold of poetry. The symbolic action involved is very clear; the writer, sensitive artificer of language, contemplates and absorbs the universe around him, transforms what he has absorbed, and returns it to the world dressed in original verbal finery. "Because a person's interior is always furnished with things from outside. The epic ends up being turned into the lyric" (*The Book of*

Esther, p. 54). His pleasure comes equally from contemplating his world and from producing his poetic versions of it.

We should note that Jarnés does not conceive of himself as the initiator of the poetic act; the stimulus must come from outside himself. Likewise, he disdains the sort of Romantic poetry-making which gives preeminent place either to the poet's internal inspiration or to the expression of idiosyncratic interests. Hence, he places strictures on literary "sincerity" which he understood as the transcription of the writer's personal problems without their first being transformed into poetry.[24]

The demand for originality implies that the writer should shun idiomatic language for it is petrified and "usually the lexicon of common sense" (*Exercises,* p. 16). Jarnés' willingness to search for a beautiful name for the thing which needs a name indicates that many attempts will often be needed before the most beautiful one is found, or before his vision finds its most satisfactory and definitive expression. He was always willing to make the logical leap if it produced a satisfactory image. The images, so often dependent upon surprising juxtapositions, are seldom extended into lengthy analogies or symbologies. Their extension would have demanded the following of the rules implicit in the initial image; Jarnés, playful and irreverent when it came to language, preferred to mock such rules. Hence, we do not find any intricate symbol systems, or sets of carefully and consistently elaborated analogies; his poetic successes are like jewels spread for examination upon a cloth, rather than like a series of matched gems set in a crown. What follows is not intended to be a full stylistic study of Jarnés' prose. We hope merely to point to some of the more conspiciuous aspects of his style and to provide a sense of its tone, point of view, and richness of texture.

Jarnés was especially fond of words denoting oscillation and movement to-and-fro. His favorite among this class was "vibration" and related terms such as "undulation, zig-zag, and vacillation."[25] Another notion of extremely high frequency in his prose is that of "shyness," especially in his male characters.[26] Both concepts are related, as we saw in the preceding section, for the artist's job is to receive the "vibrations" given off by people and things (*Sister Patrocinius,* p. 11) and transmit them in his works. Hence his protagonists, the majority of them male, must adopt a passive and contemplative stance, in order to attend to those vibrations. We might see the roots of this rather sophisticated notion in Jarnés' own description of Julio's childhood in *The Paper Guest*. Julio is at that age when everything impinges on his perception through irritations, vibrations, tremors, shivers, and tremblings on his skin (p. 9). Julio's epidermal memory is an early natural foreshadowing of the "sensitive plates" on which he will record his perceptions when an adult artist.

Just as one of Jarnés' models for the fresh and poetic expression was the child's innocent perception of the world, so too, many of his neologisms and borrowings convey a similar freshness and, at times, a childishness which stems from their surprising and often preposterous shape. We offer the following as examples: *vaselinizador,* "lubricating" (*The Red and the Blue,* p. 173); *bernardshawianos,* "Shavian" (*Paula and Paulette,* p. 43); *puzle,* "puzzle" (*ibid.,* pp. 77 and 242). We also find gallicisms, *devenir,* "to become" (*Paula and Paulette,* p. 42), and *vodevil,* "vaudeville" (*ibid.,* p. 75).

There are to be found a goodly number of neologisms made of genuine Spanish roots, words immediately understandable to the Spanish reader which probably created little stir: *transparecer,* instead of the usual *transparentar,* "to be(come) transparent" (*Scenes on the Brink of Death,* p. 10); *antiser,* "to be against" (*The Book of Esther,* p. 20); *inexistir,* "to be nonexistent" (*ibid.,* p. 130); *subcacicato,* "the rule of an under-boss" (*Sister Patrocinius,* p. 144). Words such as those cited are poetic in the fundamental sense of the word; i.e., they are newly created in order to fill a semantic gap. Though they might all be replaced, as far as their denotative meaning is concerned, with extant synonyms or circumlocutions, they are, in regard to their connotations, their subtle emanations, irreplaceable.

In the work of our author the beauties of nature play an important role. His attitude toward nature is contemplative and often he depicted man in harmonious coexistence with it. When man changed nature by imposing his manufactured stamp on it, Jarnés would satirize him pointedly (as in *Paula and Paulette),* or would heighten the contrast between nature and man by describing man's imprint in geometrical or mechanistic language. Jarnés was capable of subtle lyricism as when he writes: "The afternoon invited [him] to abandon his melancholy in its warm golden lap" (*The Red and the Blue,* p. 151); or, describing the spirits of the lake who wanted to make a little shirt for Lancelot, he could create an image worthy of and reminiscent of Lorca "To embroider for him with tiny emeralds a little shirt of foam" (*Vivien and Merlin*, p. 32). Nature was alive for Jarnés: "The last stretching of the awakening countryside could be seen in the undulations of its broad green and pale gold tunic" (*Paula and Paulette*, p. 37). The night gave off "complicated vibrations" which another Julio could classify (*Summer Salon*, p. 17).

Natural objects could react if touched by man: "The tallest pine, cupola of a little garden which bordered the road, is the most electrified. If he touched the tip of its greenblack needles, a handful of sparks would jump out; its coiled nerves would fire and the vehement balance of the whole electric countryside would be broken" (*Paula and Paulette*, pp. 68-69). The reaction of the pine is not necessarily a hostile one; we are in the midst of a much more decorous nature than we are in, for example, Rivera's *La vorágine*. And although the "vehement balance" of nature when broken could produce an electric current which Jarnés could turn into a poetic image, there is somewhat the feeling that man should not intervene in this way. Man might admire nature and, at times, derive poetic inspiration from it; but when he impressed himself upon it, the consequences might be fatal for nature. "The highway, like a dagger, plunges into the flowered bosom of the meadow where delicious breasts rise" (*ibid.*, p. 112).

When man's impact on nature is less sinister it is nonetheless antinatural. The management of the spa in *Paula and Paulette* has hidden light bulbs in the branches of the trees; when they are turned on they trace "lighted parallelograms on the blackboard of the park" (*ibid.*, p. 136). And we are told that Julio knew intimately every rock and bush in the countryside; we also find that "he could draw a picturesque map of epidermal delights . . ." which would show all the varieties of pleasure these natural features gave him (*The Paper Guest*, p. 11).

On occasion, nature is endowed with a mechancial or geometrical aspect without a character's intervention. Rather, Jarnés omits man as a causative agent of that trait: Merlin asks a man who is watching the stars if he is trying to "discover the shining telegraphy which silently governs the worlds" (*Vivien and Merlin*, p. 127). Or we find the curved lines of nature made straight: "[The sun] lazily slips through the tender orchard, through the lively reds which make the meadow a huge chessboard for the play of lights" (*The Red and the Blue,* p. 193). At times, as well, the natural and the man-made are fused into one being, alive and tempting to the hero who contemplates it, as in this picture of the city at night: "The night is a gigantic ghost with thousands of eyes pointed at Julio. Bundles of nerves, handfuls of innumerable roads which invite Julio to submerge himself in them, to look in each one for the path of delight, the track of a pleasure, the firm pulse, the open pore through which he might measure the magnificent vibration of the colossus" (*ibid.,* p. 105).

If we find natural phenomena coming alive for Jarnés because of the vibrations he can capture, we also find that man-made objects can similarly be endowed with life. As the hero contemplates suicide, he is surrounded by "hooded buildings which the darkness has just put in uniform so as to attend this simple show" (*Scenes on the Brink of Death,* p. 9). The buildings, sombrely hooded by the night, are about to witness his suicide as would a chorus of monks. The hero's mood of gloom is projected onto his physical surroundings.

In the same novel, a group of bottles comes alive as the hero awakens, arranges itself into a row, and pushes aside the papers which were on the table (*ibid.,* p. 123). Elsewhere, there are less elaborate personifications, simple and even obvious or trite ones; a train is a "powerful titan," a "formidable dragon" which lets nothing bar its way (*Paula and Paulette,* p. 25). Another example from this novel makes telegraph poles into flowers: "The telegraph, made of tree trunks and vibrations, of hard vegetable flesh through which a new sap runs, is a sort of rudimentary, schematic flower, planted by an ingenious poet" (*ibid.,* pp. 66-67). When the poet had done planting the telegraph poles, "a clever spider followed in his steps, and when it saw Spring appear through the slender masts, hastened to weave between the marvelous white buds a net that could ensnare the insects of the whole district" (*ibid.,* p. 67).

Such examples as we have just reviewed could be multiplied many times without substantially altering the impression of poetic finesse conveyed by Jarnés' prose. The imagery provides poetic texture to the quite ordinary events which surround it in the novels. But it is in the next group of examples where we find the most characteristically Jarnesian imagery, the so-called "dehumanized" images which occasioned the disdam of his critics.

In this group of images the common thread is the author's attempt to find a new shorthand for the description of commonplace acts. When he compares the thousands of individual paths of people walking in a crowded street to the paths of the stars (*Scenes on the Brink of Death*, p. 58), he is postulating a possible means of defining precisely what seem to be random movements.[27] Implicitly, he suggests that if we knew all the coordinates of each pedestrian's path, all his motives and goals, we could plot the paths of all the members of the crowd with the precision of the astronomer. By positing such a possibility, however remote, Jarnés is symbolically moving closer to the pedestrians rather than further away. Had he concluded that the movements were thoroughly random, he would symbolically have distanced himself from the crowd, for there would be no implicit gain in further contemplation of it.

There is a comparable example in his description of the hotel dining room as "a variegated mechanism, an amusing social machine, in which each part shows the signs of a different fabricating plant" (*Paula and Paulette*, p. 44). The reader is symbolically invited to examine or imagine the origins of each diner. The invitation is only symbolic, however, and it is withdrawn before the reader can accept it. For our author de-emphasized the individual backgrounds of his characters; "how they got that way" was never his primary concern. For Jarnés also, always the observer, the lives of others were like rivers and should be free of the influences of would-be reformers. The good "pure" spectator derives a deep pleasure from his observing, while the bad spectator "immediately feels the desire to correct rivers, lives, dramas" (*The Book of Esther*, p. 57).

In the description of individual characters in his novels, Jarnés often makes use of a similar geometrical or mechanical shorthand. The useless professor calls Carlota a "marvelous mechanism of pleasure" (*The Useless Professor*, p. 150). In the same novel, the professor's fingers, while he is distractedly turning the pages of a book are "docile automata" (*ibid.*, p. 19). When Vivien touches Merlin's arm, she puts him in "burning contact with the mysterious electricity of the Earth" (*Vivien and Merlin*, p. 136). When Barcelona greets the dawn it comes alive as a "geometric and vital reconstruction" (*The Red and the Blue*, p. 109).

At times, the geometry of portraiture serves to pass a negative comment on the character. In such cases, Jarnés consciously geometrizes to express contempt. The Communist cell leader, speaking to the conspirators, is described thus: "His voice progressively took on a strange tone; it was depersonalizing him, detaching itself from that mouth which was a straight line, flat, without sensuality, executive, open on the surface of a cold, imperious, inexorable face" (*ibid.*, pp. 201-2). When we see the eyes of the priest trying to restore order in his rambunctious class, they are "the double machine guns of his pupils" (*The Paper Guest*, p. 103). In both cases the mechanization or depersonalization is meant to be understood negatively. Nothing was more damnable for our author than anti-vital and rigidified authority.

Geometry is also used to desensualize a character or scene, sometimes for humorous effect. Saulo, seated at a table with six prostitute friends, contemplates their bustlines to gauge their ages by the angle at which their breasts jut out; when asked what he is doing, he replies: "Pure geometry" (*Theory of the Top-String*, p. 78).[28] Or again, when Julio is riding back to the city after rescuing Star and wrapping her naked body in a blanket, he thinks: "A lively red melody, accented by agile chords, interrupted by cascades of folds eddying about a still place—a thigh, an arm, a breast—a round surface of pure geometry" (*Summer Salon*, p. 32).

In all these examples, the primary aim is the fresh vision of beauty, often a beauty which is sculptural or plastic in outline. The emphasis on the sculptural signals the influence of a painter's vision in Jarnés' prose. For the essence of that vision is the ability to capture the relationship between forms and the spaces they fill. The mechanized imagery, modern in tone and by nature depersonalized, aims at a new approach in characterization, just as modern science has begun to make advances in the analysis of human activties previously thought unamenable to science. In our last example, after describing the varied tonalities and shadings in Esther's voice, the author says: "For there can also be a mathematics of the whisper, exact sciences of intonation, an infinitestimal calculus of shadings . . ." (*The Book of Esther,* p. 29).

Any evaluation of the place of style in Jarnés' overall output will have to await a thorough study of the style in his individual works. From our brief examination, however, certain general conclusions are apparent. What has been called his "dehumanized" prose is actually a poetic prose in which the human element is very much in evidence. If, through geometrical or mechanical imagery he endows his human characters with traits which seem inhuman, he also endows natural and inanimate objects with human or animate characteristics. We do not believe he ever overtly expressed a preference for one or the other method of characterization. Both were united as useful tools in the artist's search for new means of expression.

Enough evidence exists for us to specify the major influences and affinities with other writers in Jarnés' prose style. He admitted to great admiration for his Aragonese countrymen, Gracián and Goya.[29] We can trace the impact of Gómez de la Serna on our author, particularly the humorous and lyrical qualities of the *greguería.* Jarnés praised Unamuno's directness of style, saying that he was able to awaken the dormant vibrations in objects.[30] Undoubtedly, the Góngora Tercentenary celebrations in 1927 had an impact on Jarnés style which shares many of the traits of the Baroque poet, among them a certain labyrinthine ideation and the practise of breaking up reality into small pieces which can then be recombined in a new relationship. Jarnés praised Góngora because he exemplified intricacy in art which had taken on new prominence in the twentieth century (*Flourishes,* pp. 82 ff). Jarnés' "precious style" was said to have "outgiraudouxed Giraudoux."[31] We may also mention his admiration for Paul Valéry, whose style he thought "substantially geometrical."[32]

The fact that our author took hold of geometry for the purposes of characterization, but insisted on the need for decorative embellishment of the spare geometrical line, is apparent from his remarks on modern geometrical architecture. He called for the decoration of the pure lines of modern buildings, as well as for the adornment (*algún festón*) of prose (*The Book of Esther,* pp. 46-47). Actually, the legacy of Góngora is quite prominent in our author whose fondness for arabesques, fragmentation of reality, and for the multifaceted character we have examined above. Jarnés' suppression of anecdote and dramatic incident, his neglect of the motivations of the characters, and of the continuity of narrative themes, make it possible for us to call his style cubist.[33]

The lyrical elements of his style serve to emphasize static rather than dynamic qualities, despite the dynamism evident in words like "mechanism, trajectories," and the like. This is so because each image so described is frozen in the act; the motion is arrested by the author's need to capture the image on the photosensitive plates of the artist.[34] In addition, whereas the epic vein in poetry aims to convey dynamic action, the lyric aims to reflect the impact of a moment on the poet's sensibility. Hence, the lyricism of Jarnés' style goes hand-in-hand with the structure of his novels which do not present a connected flow of events in time, but rather collections of episodes or vignettes, each of them a lyrical perception in itself.

We should hesitate before labelling Jarnés a "dehumanized" writer. For, aside from his own hostility to dehumanization of modern life which we have described above, we should remember the preeminent place he accorded to the artist's perception, sensibility, and intelligence. Though he may describe characters with a language borrowed from technology, he never removes himself from the contemplation of those characters. Because he has observed them, assimilated them, and transmitted them to the reader through the eminently human activity of metaphorizing, the human element is always central.

CHAPTER 5

Conclusion

IN arriving at an estimation of Jarnés' importance for Spanish
literature, it is useful to recapitulate briefly the main features
of his fictional works and his characters. The uniformity of his
production in the novel over eighteen years facilitates our making
such a summary statement. It is common for historians and critics
of literature to speak of "the novels" of Jarnés. Their homogeneity
is one justification for this. Another lies in the fact that the
content of all his novels, taken individually and together, seems
to convey a similar meaning. In examining the structure of his
novels and of the fictional trajectories of his characters, we are
formulating an interpretation of the meaning of Jarnés' work as a
whole. As Octavio Paz has put it: "In art, only the forms have
meaning. The meaning is not that which the poet means to say,
but that which he in fact says. What we think we are saying
is one thing, and what we are really saying is another."[1]

We find that Jarnés' male protagonists are predominantly
passive characters. They are loath to initiate actions, they shrink
from becoming, even in the eyes of secondary characters, figures
of a heroic stature. The male protagonists are of a similar if
indeterminate age; most of them are between eighteen or twenty
and thirty-five years of age. All of them are intellectually in-
clined, and none has an unskilled occupation. But none of their
intellectual life is wholly devoted to the pursuit of any single
goal. None is writing a major work in any field, nor an epoch-
making poem or novel. They are all receptive to forms of
beauty, especially feminine beauty. Yet few of the male protagonists are married during the course of the novel. Where marriage occurs, it is either at the very end of the novel or it is
depicted as a dull, unexciting condition.

Partly because none of the male protagonists is propelled by any grand ambition, we find no violent or hostile encounters between them and other characters. There are no fights, no plots to thwart other characters' plans, no defeats for them.[2] The male protagonists do not often travel a great deal; they do a good deal of walking within the principal locale, a necessity in their restless search for new aesthetic experiences. Further, the male protagonists seldom remain long in unpleasant situations. When they are bored, suffer setbacks, or find their surroundings uncongenial, they do not attempt to rectify the matter or confront the human causes of their displeasure. They leave the scene, optimistically turning to a new trajectory for the possibilities it presents.

The female protagonists are generally stronger personalities than the males. They have fairly well defined characters. Generally they are worldly-wise seductresses (e.g., Paula, Vivien, Brunilda) who through persistence and innate charm seduce the men physically and/or spiritually. Even when the women appear initially inferior socially or intellectually, they usually undergo a certain development of physical and mental charm which helps close the distance between them and the men.

Jarnés' women frequently have multiple names or aliases, each one revealing a different facet of their personalities (e.g., Elena-Star-Carmela in *Summer Salon,* and Dolly-Isabel-Helena in *Dynamic Venus*). In addition, the female characters frequently are employed as teachers, shopclerks or dancers; none of them, with the exception of Brunilda who is a painter, is an artist or professional person. There is no hostility between the men and women characters, no war between the sexes. There are almost no clashes of wills, and the protagonists do not manipulate other characters for their own purposes. On the contrary, both sexes meet and live in harmony; once the male's reticence or reluctance is overcome, man and woman are united in the joint delights of sex and aesthetics.

Another trait common to his characters is that none of them takes a risk of any serious kind. This is a corollary of their not having any overriding ambitions. But characters who take no risks are deprived of dramatic interest, and also of the ability to create in the reader an identification with them. Jarnés thought that the creation of dramatism in the novel was a sort of pandering to the low tastes of a mass public.[3] In adopting

Ortega's dictum against the fostering of the reader's identification with the character, Jarnés, the "pure" spectator, wanted to address himself to a reader molded in his own image.

We meet the characters of Jarnés' novels when they are mature or almost mature adults, and seldom learn anything about their childhoods. Since there are no grand ambitions, there are no important motivations. Similarly, few of the characters die at the end of the novel, hence their trajectories are unfinished, subject to prolongation in subsequent novels or in enlarged versions of the same novel. This is why we called the novels open-ended. While this quality saves the characters from failure to attain goals, it also keeps them from success. Jarnés disliked the neatly contrived plot and particularly the dramatic climax; he thought them unlifelike and we seldom find the "well-told-tale" in his works.

And despite the standing invitation to the reader to imagine his own end to the novel, to participate in it, the reader feels that the novel is insubstantial. Since there are hardly any conflicts, there are no resolutions. The open-ended structure implies a lack of structure both in the character and in the plot in the Jarnesian novel. For if the character and plot are not rounded off, then implicit problems in the novel have not been solved. Social and political problems may be treated in the novels—Marxism in *The Red and the Blue,* apostasy in *The Paper Guest* —but they are not given fundamental importance in the character. Hence, they do not really matter to the reader.

Another trait common to almost all of Jarnés' novels is their unitary theme: the sensitive artist as recorder of the beauty around him. While it is true that different novels provide somewhat different versions of beauty, it is also true that the method of looking never changes. Because Jarnés' characters are devoid of sentimentality and often enough of sentiment as well, they convey an impression of impermanence. They all take a similarly detached stance before the world, and they are all concerned with the sensory appearances of things. As we have mentioned, the characters in the novels are not in the process of "becoming," but are rather in various states of "being." Since the themes and characters show no particular development, either within a given work or over the whole of his production, it is probably academic to speak of a development of the novelistic art of

Jarnés. He did not set himself any problems to solve in his work, hence the works do not themselves progress (or regress) from one set of solutions to another.

The predominant impression we receive from Jarnés' novels is that their author viewed the world around him as one in a state of flux and fluidity, a world where all things were related to one another, where life obeys an imperative of continuity. The novels are open-ended; they are devoid of dramatic incident or climax. His characters refuse to initiate or terminate, to be the "prime mover." If in fact Jarnés thought climax anti-vital, if he saw beginnings and endings as but transitions of little intrinsic importance between various links in a "great chain of being," then notions of a developmental sort—either applied to his characters or to the novels—would indeed have mattered little to him.

We may point to certain parallels between the author's life and his work. We know that Jarnés was seldom involved in hostile confrontations with antagonists. Where he found a situation uncongenial, his response was to leave it (e.g., the church, the army, Franco Spain).[4] Jarnés' life, as much as the lives of any of his co-generationists, was marked by many discontinuities, mainly of occupation and of residence. His novels, likewise, are discontinuous both because of their episodic nature, and because of the lack of thematic unity from one work to another.

In addition, the marked emphasis on originality in Jarnés' criticial writings reflect his insecurities about his own literary worth, as well as his conviction that repetition was useless in art. Hence, we find in his production a considerable number of works which, although original in their presentation of ever-new visions of beauty, are repetitive in their method, characterizations and style.

Jarnés' notion of originality, in other words, was one oriented to the externals, to the mere fact of priority of existence in time. This sort of originality is objective, and it can be shown that no one else had written of the spa at Alhama as he had in *Paula and Paulette*. Yet, there is another sort of originality, one we might call self-oriented, which perhaps would have yielded more enduring novels for our author.

For if he had been convinced that whatever was original with him in his own life history was indeed original, whether it had been written or had existed before, he would have been led toward increased self-confidence and toward an emphasis on the development of his art. Naturally the demand for originality carries with it a demand for continual change; yet, as we have noted, by the early 1930's his inventive fertility had largely disappeared, and his work after that time seems increasingly repetitive. Hence, by his own definition, his work in the novel becomes useless in the 1930's.

Another characteristic which unites his life and his work is the multitude of different outlets which he found for his numerous production. Novels, essays, plays, short stories, critical articles, book reviews, and biographies appeared under his name in a profusion of reviews, newspapers, and publishing houses. Such a voluminous and varied output again implies restlessness and a search for originality. Each of the genres he cultivated offers a slightly different view of the author, although in each we perceive the same author. What Jarnés admired most in Joyce's Stephen Dedalus was that he was not one single personality, but a whole gallery of portraits of personality (*Flourishes*, p. 35). Reading Jarnés' own work we get a similar impression. The stress is not on the underlying unity of personality, but on the multifaceted variety of which the personality is capable. For Jarnés the former represented limitation and rigidity, while the latter represented freedom.

Undoubtedly Jarnés embodies in the Spain of the 1920's and 1930's tendencies and movements of lasting literary importance. He contributed to the writing of novels an intelligence and a subtlety of language and innovative perspectives which have begun to make their appearance again in Spanish authors. He served an important function, through his many book reviews of European and American authors, of helping to keep Spain *au courant* in literary matters. His alertness to the importance of cinema and its potential influence on literature was a timely and valuable contribution; his use of Teutonic and Classical myths was equally important. Together with certain other prose writers (Espina, Marichalar, Chacel), Jarnés opened new possibilities for the novel. The importance of his group for prose is perhaps analogous with an American group with whom there were certain affinities—the Algonquin Round Table.[5]

While Jarnés' artistic credo in the 1920's that the categorical imperative of art is sensuality (*Ariel in Flight*, p. 105) might have escaped serious condemnation, his continued adherence to the same position in the 1930's was to evoke censure from several quarters. Censure came first from those whose democratic leanings caused them to disparage the Jarnesian and Orteguian emphasis on the aristocracy of literature.[6] Secondly, those who sought in the novel either an attempt to solve real-life problems or, at the least, characters with whom they could identify, found the stylistic subtlety and the emphasis on the sensuous and voluptuous surfaces of things disappointing. A third group thought Jarnés' works were detached exercises which dispensed with the visible world around him. In their case, their criticism was wrong-headed. For as we have seen, the novels are full of visible Spanish reality, and the author's liberal thinking on matters of national concern can be found in every novel he wrote. What this group of critics is probably responding to is their discovery that such matters of vital national concern were made, in Jarnés' fictions, into pretexts or backgrounds for esthetic play.

Lastly, Jarnés has been criticized by those whose understanding of the world around them demanded a writer of more complexity and depth. In the 1930's literary discussion had reached an extreme degree of politicization. Jarnés' hallmark, intelligence, could serve the world of letters well enough in a time of cultural and artistic innovation and freedom. But at mid-decade, intelligence was not enough. We need but recall General Millán Astray's infamous expostulation, "Down with intelligence! Long live death!" at the University of Salamanca in September, 1936, to see that the viability of letters in Spain had come to depend upon weapons. Intelligence had become a luxury for both sides in the Civil War.

As we saw above (p. 127), Jarnés' grasp of the problems of the human condition in his age at times fell short of its elusive and subtle complexities. Where Jarnés formulated the major problem of his age as the war between profit and grace, and called for human beings to be generous with each other, there were some, like André Malraux, who were writing of Spain in utterly different terms: "Once more in this land of black-clothed women, as so often in the past, a generation of widows was in the making. When such things are being done, what is the meaning of 'nobility'? Or 'generosity'?"[7]

In this introductory study we have reached a certain perspective on Jarnés' work and contribution to the Spanish novel. The fact that the production of the poets of his Generation has mostly overshadowed the works of the novelists makes it perhaps more difficult to arrive at a balanced evaluation of Jarnés. When further investigations have been made into his novelistic art, his use of language, his contact with other writers of his Generation, both Spanish and foreign, we believe they will show that Jarnés occupied, in the decade and a half before the Civil War, a preeminent position in the Spanish novel.

Notes and References

Throughout this book page numbers in parentheses in the text refer to the work under immediate discussion except where otherwise indicated.

Chapter One

1. Benjamín Jarnés, unpublished "Notebook No. 21," quoted in Víctor Fuentes, "La obra de Benjamín Jarnés: Un estudio de su novelística y de su estética," unpublished Ph.D. thesis, New York University, 1965, p. 48, n. 2. Here, as elsewhere in this study, translations from the Spanish are my own unless otherwise specified.

2. Benjamín Jarnés, "Años de aprendizaje y alegría," prologue to *Viviana y Merlín* (Madrid: Ediciones Ulises, 1930), p. 18. The reader will find Jarnés' published books listed in the bibliography.

3. Carmen Irizarry, *The Thirty Thousand* (New York: Harcourt, Brace and World, 1966), gives an account of the precarious religious freedom enjoyed by Spanish Protestants in this century.

4. "Años de aprendizaje y alegría," p. 15.

5. Unpublished "Notebook No. 24," quoted in Fuentes, *op. cit.*, p. 49, n. 1.

6. In the editorial note preceding the *Enciclopedia de la literatura,* which Jarnés edited (México: Editora Central [1947], I, 9), we learn that his family was too poor to provide elementary education for him. So he began his studies at the university at the age of ten.

7. Unpublished "Notebook No. 11," quoted in Fuentes, *op. cit.*, p. 53, n. 2. On his motives for leaving the seminary he had this to say: "Do I know the reason? I have never known it. Now that belongs to my deeper life, so deep that I—who have approached it very often—have not been able to make it out. . . . I went from one world to another, happily, without anyone's rejecting me in the first one or anything's inviting me into the second."

8. Fuentes, *op. cit.*, p. 55. Fuentes, because he consulted Jarnés' widow, should probably be considered accurate. Germán Bleiberg

thought that Jarnés joined the service with the rank of lieutenant (*Diccionario de literatura española* [Madrid: Revista de Occidente, 3rd rev. ed., 1964], p. 425). This would seem unlikely considering the makeup of the officer corps in the Spanish army and Jarnés' humble family background. See Gerald Brenan, *The Spanish Labyrinth* (Cambridge: Cambridge University Press, 1960), pp. 60-61. Eugenio de Nora says that Jarnés rose to lieutenant only in 1930, and to captain in 1936 (*La novela española contemporánea* [Madrid: Gredos, 1962], II, 151, n. 1.).

9. Cf. Brenan, *op. cit.*, p. 61.

10. It is to be hoped that Fuentes will in time make available whatever he was able to learn from Doña Gregoria Bergua, Jarnés' widow, that may help fill in these gaps.

11. Fuentes, *op. cit.*, p. 57, n. 3, says that the articles in *El Pilar* were angry attacks on Modernism and its derivative movements.

12. Ricardo Gullón ("Benjamín Jarnés," *Insula*, IV, 46 [15 October, 1949], p. 8), writes that the priest in question was the author's brother, Pedro.

13. Jarnés ("Años de aprendizaje y alegría," pp. 26-27) says that the way in which he happened to join Ortega's review is told by Valentín Andrés Alvarez in the preface to his *Naufragio en la sombra*. In that "Apunte autobiográfico" to his novel (Madrid: Ediciones Ulises, 1930), p. 19, Andrés Alvarez says that Manuel García Morente was the one to bring to Ortega's attention the pieces of his and Jarnés' which had appeared in *Plural*. García Morente was a friend of Ortega's and long-time secretary of the *Revista de Occidente*.

14. From unpublished "Notebook No. 10," Spring, 1933, quoted in Fuentes, *op. cit.*, p. 68, n. 4.

15. Gullión, *art. cit.*, p. 8.

16. The book was Guillermo de Torre's *Literaturas europeas de vanguardia* (Madrid: Caro Raggio, 1925). "Años de aprendizaje y alegría," p. 21.

17. *Ibid.*, p. 23.

18. *Ibid.*, p. 26. In 1929, a literary banquet was held to celebrate the appearance of *El convidado de papel* (*The Paper Guest*). Among those present were Azorín, Gómez de la Serna, Fernando Vela, Antonio Espina, and Giménez Caballero. The latter said: "Benjamín Jarnés is not a touchy or aggressive man. . . . His aggression: talent. His defense: modesty." Quoted in *ibid.*, p. 28.

19. Jaime Torres Bodet, *Tiempo de arena*, in *Obras escogidas* (México: Fondo de Cultura Económica, 1961), p. 376. Among those present on this occasion were Pedro Salinas, Antonio Marichalar, Rafael Alberti, and José Bergamín.

20. They are presumably in the possession of Jarnés' widow. Fuentes, *op. cit.*, p. 64, n. 1.

21. Unpublished "Notebook No. 5," quoted in *ibid.*, p. 72, n. 2.

22. Jarnés, *Cita de ensueños* (Madrid: Galo Sáez, 1936).

23. The objective, so often associated with Ortega, of Europeanizing Spain, was acknowledged even in 1930 to have been achieved, at least so far as culture was concerned. See Darío Pérez, *Figuras de España* (Madrid: Compañía Ibero-Americana de Publicaciones, 1930), p. 277.

24. We do not know what precise responsibilities Jarnés held during his Army service in these years. He is reported to have said that he was compiling statistics on the production of chickens in Spain. See Eduardo de Ontañón, *Viaje y aventura de los escritores de España* (México: Ediciones Minerva [1942]), p. 184.

25. Fuentes, *op. cit.*, pp. 73-74. Of *Ruins* one fragment was published: "Ruinas en España," *Hora de España* [Valencia], 16 (1938), 71-78.

26. Ontañón, *op. cit.*, p. 189.

27. There is as yet no thorough treatment of the exiles as a group. However, the interested reader should consult: Isabel de Palencia, *Smouldering Freedom* (New York and Toronto: Longmans, Green, 1945), Carlos Martínez, *Crónica de una emigración* (México: Libro Mex, 1959); José R. Marra-López, *Narrativa española fuera de España: 1939-1961* (Madrid: Guadarrama, 1963).

28. Jarnés arrived in Mexico in June, 1939 (Ontañón, p. 181). On 13 September 1939, his *Cardenio* was presented in the Teatro Orientación by the Dramatic Club of the Institute of Fine Arts in Mexico City.

29. He told Ontañón that he was forced by economic necessity to undertake all sorts of writing assignments, from detective stories to reviews of concerts. In 1940, La Casa de España en México asked him for a book which was published as *Cartas al Ebro;* also Xavier Villaurrutia asked him for another, the novel *La novia del viento*. He referred to yet another book which was to appear under Bergamín's Editorial Séneca imprint, but which was "lost in the press." See Ontañón, pp. 186-87.

30. Cf. Emilia de Zuleta, "Benjamín Jarnés," *Universidad* [Santa Fe, Argentina], LV (1963), 46. Jarnés recognized this motive in the biographical writing of Stefan Zweig, and we have no reason to believe that it was not also a motive of his own biographical works. Speaking of Zweig's numerous biographies, he wrote that Zweig was "a writer of our time who suffers the great concerns of the present day, to the point of not being able to stand them, to the point of evading them for once and for all" by writing about the lives of people who had

lived before his time *(Stefan Zweig: cumbre apagada, retrato* [México: Editorial Proa, 1942], p. 147). Perhaps one of the roots of the evasive impulse in his writing can be seen in the notebooks which he kept during the war; they were full of notes which did not deal with the war. "They were my escape hatch into other, more pleasant worlds, sometimes chimerical, inaccessible ones. . . . I have never given my fantasy such free rein as during the war . . ." (Quoted in Ontañón, p. 190).

31. Guillermo de Torre, "La emigración intelectual, drama contemporáneo" [1940], in *Tríptico del sacrificio* (Buenos Aires: Losada, 2nd ed., 1960), p. 133.

32. Fuentes, *op. cit.*, p. 78.

33. Cf. Ricardo Gullón, "Inventario de medio siglo: II. Literatura española," *Insula*, V, 58 (15 October, 1950), 6. If the exiles' works were not always subject to official Spanish press censorship, they were frequently issued by small publishing houses without extensive distribution facilities, and did not reach Spain at all. In fact, in Spain even today most of the works of Jarnés are to be found, if at all, at the rare book sellers' where they are treated in much the same way as *Lady Chatterly's Lover* and *Tropic of Cancer* were treated in the U.S. before 1958. And Jarnés' books were neither considered pornographic nor were they overtly hostile to the Franco regime.

34. The editors of *Las Españas*, a literary and cultural review published in Mexico City, wrote in an obituary note: "Benjamín Jarnés, famous writer and dear friend, has died. . . . Sick and unaware of his surroundings, he was taken to Spain; but his spirit and his will shall remain in exile" [José Ramón Arana and Manuel Andújar, "Benjamín Jarnés," *Las Españas*, V, 13 (29 October 1949), 3.

Chapter Two

1. "Prólogo" to the *Enciclopedia de la literatura* edited by Jarnés (México: Editora Central [1947]), I, 11.

2. This Generation in Spanish literature is variously dated as of the year 1925 or 1927. We shall refer to it with the latter date, the year of the Góngora tercentenary which evoked and crystallized many of the attitudes of the vanguard writers of the time. Combining novelists and essayists, Ricardo Gullón lists the following prose writers of the Generation: Dámaso Alonso, Valentín Andrés Alvarez, Max Aub, Francisco Ayala, Mauricio Bacarisse, José Bergamín, José María de Cossío, Juan Chabás, Antonio Espina, Melchor Fernández Almagro, Ernesto Giménez Caballero, Jarnés, Antonio Marichalar, Adolfo Salazar, Pedro Salinas, Guillermo de Torre, Claudio de la Torre, and Fernando Vela ("Prosistas de la generación del '25," *Insula*, XII, 126 [15 May 1957], 1). I would suggest the addition of two others: Rosa Chacel and Esteban Salazar y Chapela.

3. An excellent summary of the situation in Europe in these years is found in Guillermo de Torre, *Historia de las literaturas de vanguardia* (Madrid: Guadarrama, 1965), esp. pp. 317-609.

4. Germán Bleiberg and Julián Marias, eds., *Diccionario de literatura española, s. v.,* "Poetas españoles actuales."

5. José Francisco Cirre, *Forma y espíritu de una lírica española: Noticia sobre la renovación poética en España de 1920 a 1935* (México: Gráfica Panamericana, 1950), pp. 44-45.

6. See, e.g., *Ejercicios* (Madrid: Cuadernos Literarios, 1927), pp. 80-83. In 1925, he had called Ortega a "sage exegete of the novel." "[Review of] Ramón Gómez de la Serna, *La quinta de Palmira,*" *Revista de Occidente* (hereafter *RO*), X, 28 (1925), 114.

7. "Nota preliminar, *Paula y Paulita* (Madrid: Revista de Occidente, 1929), p. 19. In *El profesor inútil* he cites Emerson in regard to his belief that "art should be a veil through which total human energy harmoniously flows" (Madrid: Espasa-Calpe, new ed., 1934), p. 90.

8. "Libros sin género," *RO*, XXXII, 95 (1931), 207.

9. Esteban Salazar y Chapela, "Literatura plana y literatura del espacio," *RO*, XV, 44 (1927), 283.

10. Other members of the Generation thought, with Jarnés, that innovation, creativity, and orginality were, by definition, productive of aesthetic beauty. For example, Antonio Espina believed it essential for the writer to innovate, "that is, *create* in order to achieve his beautiful effects" (*El nuevo diantre* [Madrid: Espasa-Calpe, 1934], p. 23).

11. Fourteen years later, Jarnés was to express a somewhat different opinion. In a postscript to a book of poems by Manuel Delgado, he praised the poet for being a tireless artisan, a lover of the Classical myths, and a cultivator of traditional rhythms in poetry. He spoke highly of Delgado's having renounced all those so common rebellions usually found in modern books of poetry. See "Posdata" to Delgado's *Reloj de arena* (México: Biblioteca Hoy, 1941), pp. 145-46. It is likely that this change of opinion was due in part to the effect of the experience of the Civil War and World War II, for he considered war as a primary example of rebelliousness.

12. "De estrategia literaria," *RO*, XXX, 90 (1930), 373.

13. Quoted by Hugo Rodríguez-Alcalá, "Un aspecto del antagonismo de Unamuno y Ortega," *Revista de la Universidad de Buenos Aires*, II (1957), 275.

14. Mariano Baquero Goyanes, *Problemas de la novela contemporánea* (Madrid: Ateneo, 2nd ed., 1956), p. 16.

15. Quoted in Armando E. Zubizarreta, *Unamuno en su nivola* (Madrid: Taurus, 1960), p. 332, n. 56.

16. Cf. Doris King Arjona, "*La voluntad* and *abulia* in Contemporary Spanish Ideology," *Revue Hispanique*, LXXIV (1928), 645. Also,

Segundo Serrano Poncela, "Razón y débito a Ortega y Gasset," in *El secreto de Melibea* (Madrid: Taurus, 1956), p. 214.

17. "Respuesta a Ortega," *Sur*, 241 (1956), 96-119.

18. See Francisco Ayala, "Proemio [1949]," in *La cabeza del cordero* (Buenos Aires: Compañía General Fabril Editora, 1962), p. 30.

19. "Le temps, la distance et la forme chez Proust," *La Nouvelle Revue Française*, X, 113 (1923), 269.

20. In *Obras completas* (Madrid: Revista de Occidente, 1947), III, 360.

21. *Ideas sobre la novela*, p. 389.

22. "Ensayo de estética a manera de prólogo" [1914], in *Obras completas* (Madrid: Revista de Occidente, 1961), VI, 263.

23. The distinction is made by Percy Lubbock, *The Craft of Fiction* [1912] (New York: Viking Press, 1960), esp. pp. 110-23.

24. E. M. Forster, *Aspects of the Novel* [1924] (New York: Harcourt, Brace, 1954), p. 86. According to Foster, "The king died and then the queen died," is a story; "the king died, and then the queen died of grief," is a plot.

25. As has often been pointed out, Ortega's comments apply better to painting than they do to literature. The physical nature of the two art forms provide their first points of differentiation. A painting is set in a frame which separates it from everything else in its environment. It is displayed in a museum, at a discreet distance from other paintings, in order to be looked at by a spectator from some distance. It is not ordinarily portable or easily handled. Books, of course, are more accessible; great works may stand next to poor ones on a shelf. Books may be found in the humblest home or the one where there has been a lack of education. In his remarks on literature, Ortega is trying to claim for books some of the exclusivity of painting. He is invoking a sort of awe on the part of the reader who should feel himself in the presence of great art no less when reading a great book than when viewing a great painting. In this vein Jarnés gives us the clue for this interpretation of Ortega's meaning: "literature should be presented as a show *(espectáculo)*" ("Prólogo" to his *Enciclopedia de la literatura* [México: Editora Central, 1947], I, 12).

With all that the word "show" connotes—the theater, the performance of skilled actors within the frame of apron, walls and proscenium arch, the presence of spectators at a certain remove from the stage, the imitation of real life tempered or distorted by the dramatist's art—we see Jarnés' basic aim for literature. In addition, the mechanics of the play or "show," the technical arrangements for sets, costumes and makeup, are hidden from the audience and are not—at least at this date in Spain—made very much a tangible part of the performance. They are part of the "mystery" of the play, understood by and important to the initiated only.

26. "Ensayo de estética a manera de prólogo," p. 250.

27. "Prólogo casi doctrinal sobre la novela," in *Obras completas* (Madrid: Bibliotcca Nueva, 1948), IV, 313.

28. "Fe de erratas" [1926], in *Cartas al Ebro* (México: La Casa de España en México, 1940), p. 31.

29. Ciriaco Morón Arroyo, "Algebra y logoritmo: Dos metáforas de Ortega y Gasset," *Hispania*, XLIX (1966), 233.

30. Rosa Chacel, "Respuesta a Ortega," p. 101.

31. On the threshold of this period, Salaverría thought that art was in the paradox of being democratic during aristocratic periods and of tending toward the esoteric and aristocratic during a time of universal suffrage. José María Salaverría, *La intimidad literaria* (Madrid: Ed. Calleja, 1919), p. 112.

32. Cf. Franciso Ayala; "Proemio," p. 30: "The new generation showed itself to be very detached from immediate realities, through aesthetic attitudes which aspired to the maximum distance with regard to the social milieu."

33. Marshall McLuhan, "Third Program in the Human Age," *Explorations*, 8 (1957), 17. Cf. Antonio Espina who, using a comparison which was also a favorite of Jarnés', wrote that the author "is the sensitive antenna of all kinds of new and old representations; the new and the new-born ones which still have no name, and the old ones which are scrupulously recorded in the dictionary" (*El nuevo diantre*, p. 23).

34. "Una novela," in *Cartas al Ebro*, pp. 90-91. Jarnés depended upon real life to provide him with living characters and also to help him define his own individuality: "Thus it is necessary to plunge into Humanity so that it can tune us up, serve as a mirror in which to see how shy and out of tune we are" (*Libro de Esther* [Madrid: Espasa-Calpe, 1935], p. 41).

35. Marra López, *Narrativa española* . . ., p. 30.

36. Nora, *La novela española* . . ., II, 188.

37. "The Modern Spanish Novel," tr. Douglas M. Rogers, *Texas Quarterly*, IV (1961), 87.

38. "Una polémica sobre la 'Deshumanización del arte,' " in *El fiel de la balanza* (Madrid: Taurus, 1961), p. 77.

39. "Ensayo de estética a manera de prólogo," p. 249.

40. Juan Chabás, *Literatura española contemporánea: 1898-1950* (La Habana: Ed. Cultural, 1952), pp. 367-68.

41. Aub, *Discurso de la novela española contemporánea* (México: El Colegio de México, 1945), p. 81.

42. Zuleta, "Benjamín Jarnés," *Universidad*, LV (1963), 48.

152   BENJAMÍN JARNÉS

43. S[egundo] Serrano Poncela, "La novela española contemporánea," *La Torre,* I (1953), 110.

44. Nora, *op. cit.,* II, 158.

45. *Attitudes Toward History* (Boston: Beacon Press, 1961), p. 318.

46. Albert Camus, *Notebooks,* tr. Philip Thody (New York: Knopf, 1963), p. 71, n. 3.

47. Rosa Chacel, "Respuesta a Ortega," p. 107.

48. Jarnés had expressed a similar notion in 1931. See "Libros sin género" (cf. n. 8, chap. 2), p. 206.

49. Cf. Wayne C. Booth, *The Rhetoric of Fiction* (Chicago and London: Chicago University Press, 1961), pp. 119-21.

50. Ayala, "Proemio" (cf. n. 18, chap. 2), p. 29. Ultimately, the question of how gratuitous a work is depends upon the reader's point of view. In discussing this problem, Guillermo de Torre posits a "disinterested literature" as the opposite of "committed literature." He comments that "in no way should this disinterest be understood to imply gratuity, and much less irresponsibility of the writer or artist in his time and before his environment, since irresponsibility is unthinkable" *(Problemática de la literatura* [Buenos Aires: Losada, 2nd ed., 1958], p. 170.

51. See Malcolm Cowley, *Exile's Return* (New York: Viking, 1956), p. 304, for comments on the situation in America.

52. "Benjamín Jarnés: *Libro de Esther,*" RO, XLVIII, 142, (1935), 111.

53. Quoted from an interview in *El Sol* [Madrid], 10 June 1936, by Guillermo de Torre, *Tríptico del sacrificio,* p. 70.

54. Charles L. King, "Sender's Spherical Philosophy," *Publications of the Modern Language Association,* (hereafter PMLA), LXIX (1954), 994. Also, Ricardo Gullón, "Inventario de medio siglo: II, Literatura española" (cf. n. 33, chap. 1), p. 3.

55. Ayala, "Proemio" (cf. n. 18, chap. 2), p. 31.

56. Rosa Chacel, "Respuesta a Ortega," p. 109.

57. Guillermo de Torre, "Las ideas estéticas de Ortega," *Sur,* 241 (1956), 85.

58. David I. Grossvogel, *Limits of the Novel* (Ithaca: Cornell University Press, 1968), p. 279.

59. The Orteguian aesthetic position, as well as that of Surrealism, had been substantially eroded by the war. The startling and intentionally offensive imagery of the Surrealists, the involvement in artistry and mechanized imagery of writers who shared Jarnés' persuasion, had been superseded for once and all by the terror of gas chambers and

the fatal ingenuity exercised during both the Spanish Civil War and World War II. Cf. Guillermo de Torre, *Problemática de la literatura,* 2nd ed., p. 286.

Chapter Three

1. The other works in the series "Nova Novarum" were: in 1926, Pedro Salinas, *Vísperas del gozo;* in 1927, Antonio Espina, *Pájaro pinto;* and in 1929, Jarnés, *Paula y Paulita,* Espina, *Luna de copas,* and Valentín Andrés Alvarez, *Tararí.*

2. Nora, *La novela española,* II, 166, says that from Jarnés' initial concept of the "artistic novel" embodied in *El profesor inútil* until his last works, "no evolution, no considerable change of attitude can be shown."

3. Nueva (2a) edición (Madrid: Espasa-Calpe, 1934). The preface, "Discurso a Herminia," dates from 1933. The added story is "Zoco y bodegón," and the epilogue is titled, "En resumen." All citations from this novel are from this 2nd edition.

4. Víctor Fuentes, "La obra de Benjamín Jarnés," p. 138, n. 2.

5. "Años de aprendizaje y alegría," pp. 9 and 14.

6. Fuentes, op. cit., p. 132.

7. "La musa de ébano," *RO,* XVIII, 52 (1927), 111.

8. The error of those who attacked Jarnés for being a Surrealist is obvious. See, e.g., Juan José Domenchina, *Crónicas de Gerardo Rivera* (México: Ed. Centauro, 2nd ed., 1946) p. 105.

9. Madrid: Historia Nueva. The text bears the date 1924. A second edition was issued (Madrid: Espasa-Calpe, 1935). All quotations are from the first edition.

10. See Ildefonso Manuel Gil, "Ciudades y paisajes aragoneses en las novelas de Benjamín Jarnés," *Archivo de Filología Aragonesa,* VI (1956), 87-114.

11. Jarnés knew this novel of Joyce's, most likely in the Spanish translation which he reviewed when it appeared. See "James Joyce: *El artista adolescente,*" *RO,* XIII, 39 (1926), 382-86.

12. "Familiarity kills attentiveness: we only attend well to that which is a bit distant" (p. 10). Jarnés' insistence on the need for distance is one of the causes of the absence of "socially committed" themes or viewpoints in his work. It leads his critics to accuse him of detachment from the vital problems of the Spain of his day.

13. Madrid: Revista de Occidente.

14. *RO,* X, 29 (1925), 129-60. There is an indication that Jarnés planned a second edition of *Paula y Paulita* which, however, did not appear. In Fuentes' opinion (*op. cit.* in note 1, chap. 1) the story, "Bílbilis," which appeared in *El Hijo Pródigo,* V, 16 (1944), 26-31, was intended for this second edition.

15. Nora, *La novela española* . . ., II, 170, remarks on the resemblances between this novel and Gabriel Miró's *Las cerezas del cementerio* [1910].

16. He is called "Professor, useless professor" (p. 162).

17. *Stefan Zweig*, p. 28.

18. Madrid: Ed. Oriente. The first four chapters had previously appeared in *RO*, XIX, 35 (1928), 1-39. The second edition, from the 1937 revision made by Jarnés and provided by his widow, appeared in Joaquín de Entrambasaguas, ed., *Las mejores novelas contemporáneas* (Barcelona: Planeta, 1961), VII, 1379-1564.

19. The first edition, with ten chapters, has rather fewer secondary characters and less plot action than the second, which has twenty. But the thematic concern is equally prominent in both. The second edition should be considered definitive, since it was revised by the author himself. Those interested in some of the details of the changes in the second edition may consult Fuentes, *op. cit.*, pp. 191-99.

20. Nora, *op. cit.*, II, 171-72.

21. See Paul Ilie, "Benjamín Jarnés: Aspects of the Dehumanized Novel," *PMLA*, LXXVI (1961), 247-53.

22. Madrid: Espasa-Calpe, 1930.

23. In an interesting, recent study, Paul Ilie elicits evidence of the author's Surrealistic manner from this novel of Jarnés' *(The Surrealistic Mode in Spanish Literature* [Ann Arbor: The University of Michigan Press, 1968], esp. pp. 156-171). It would seem that despite our author's use of Surrealistic devices in various of his works, his allegiance to Surrealism as a primary source for his novelistic technique was only sporadic, and tended to diminish after the early 1930's. Jarnés granted too much importance to the role of a consciousness as a censor for his adherence to Surrealism to be more than a flirtation. Also, in Jarnés' view, Surrealism's debt to Freud implied reliance upon unconscious sources for fiction; this was a reliance Jarnés found highly uncongenial. Jarnés' attitude toward Freudianism continued to be as hostile late in his career as it had been earlier. In the article on Freud in his *Enciclopedia de la literatura*, we read that "Freud is the inventor of the *subconscious:* a sort of little beast or devil which we all carry inside and which only makes itself known indirectly and in a disguised way" (II, 753). On at least one question, however, Jarnés and Freud shared a similar opinion. In *Stefan Zweig*, Jarnés equated civilization with force, violence, and mechanization, while he thought culture was synonymous with life, happiness, ingenuity, and humor; he agreed with Spengler that "civilization is the fatal outcome of any culture" (pp. 114-15). We should remember that Freud had expressed a similar opinion in a book which Jarnés probably did not know, *Civilization and Its Discontents*.

24. Madrid: Espasa-Calpe.

25. We find the narrator employing the usual Jarnesian appellation when he tells Isabel: "I'm a useless professor for you" (p. 64). He later adds: "I'm not a man of passion. I'm a neurotic!" (p. 66). Fuentes *(op. cit.,* p. 215), mentions the bitterness and disappointment which pervade Jarnés' writings at the beginning of the 1930's.

26. Madrid: Espasa-Calpe.

27. Jarnés' admiration for Stendhal was a long-standing one, to judge from *The Paper Guest*. In that novel, one of the books secretly passed from student to student was Stendhal's novel. Nora, *(op. cit.,* II, 153), says Jarnés was devoted to Julien Sorel with whom he felt a "deep spiritual fraternity."

28. Like other Jarnesian heroes, this Julio is given a number. In the instance at hand, however, the hero is "a tactical element" in addition to being a number. Therefore, he is not entirely depersonalized; he will be used *by* someone *for* some purpose. Of course, his being used by someone indicates clearly enough the passivity of his character. We should also note that his numerical identity falls away as soon as he begins to interact with other characters. He is not addressed or referred to with his number throughout the novel, nor does he address his fellow recruits with their numbers. Despite his general passivity as a character, when he relates to the other characters he does so, not as a number, but as a person.

29. On the final page of *Cita de ensueños (A Date with Illusion)* (p. 158), *The Red and the Blue* is listed as a sequel to *The Paper Guest*. *Scenes on the Brink of Death* is listed as a sequel to *The Useless Professor*.

30. Madrid: La Gaceta Literaria

31. Madrid: Ediciones Ulises, 1930. The second edition, illustrated by Luisa Butler, was published in Madrid by Espasa-Calpe in 1936. All quotations from this work are from the second edition.

32. *La novia del viento* was published in Mexico: Editorial Cultura, 1940.

33. México: Editorial Proa, 1943.

34. Madrid: Editores Reunidos, 1936. This novelette appeared as the fourteenth in a weekly series called "The One-Hour Novel." Authors of other titles in the series were: Palacio Valdés, W. Fernández Flórez, Pedro Mata, Manuel Bueno, Concha Espina, Eduardo Zamacois, Jardiel Poncela, J. M. Salaverría, Alberto Insúa, Francisco Camba, J. M. Pemán, Cristóbal de Castro, and Mariano Tomás who also edited the series. Forthcoming works were to be by Luis Araquistáin, Pío Baroja, and Emilio Carrere.

35. *Crónica de una emigración,* pp. 222-23.

36. *Problemática de la literatura,* 2nd ed., p. 193.

Chapter Four

1. *Cartas al Ebro*, pp. 168-69.

2. In his review of Gerhard Hauptman's *La prodigiosa isla de las damas (RO*, X, 29 [1925], 249), he wrote: "A people is nothing without a mythic past . . ."

3. Reviewing Karl Dietrich's *Figuras bizantinas*, Jarnés wrote of how "useless an enterprise it is always to humble ourselves before the past." "Estambul, la sinuosa" (*RO*, XIX, 56 [1928]), 293.

4. On the eve of the Spanish Civil War he wrote: "Instincts are getting together, closing ranks. Instincts dancing—here is the whole of modern politics . . ." *Don Alvaro o la fuerza del tino* (Madrid: Editores Reunidos, [12 June] 1936), p. 26.

5. "[Review of] Jean Giraudoux, *Bella*," *RO*, XII, 34 (1926), 115.

6. The position of political moderate was shared by many members of the Generation, among them Antonio Espina who, in 1934, responding to the Republic's failure successfully to deal with social and political problems, had written: "But the Republic which does not channel and contain those great proletarian movements which are fighting for a just cause has no reason for existing at this stage" (*El nuevo diantre*, p. 91).

7. *Escuela de libertad* (México: Ed. Continental, 1942), pp. 17-18.

8. Critics who charge Jarnés with failure to attend to political reality have probably overlooked such passages as his sketch of Dolores Ibarruri, "La Pasionaria"; he wrote: "The old revolutionary who has the name of a flower comes in [to the Ateneo]. Smiling, she asks for a book and sits down to enjoy some futurist panoramas, full of opulent words with capital letters: Love, Pity, Freedom . . ." *Escenas junto a la muerte*, p. 34.

9. See, e.g., Richard Crossman, ed., *The God That Failed* (London: Hamish Hamilton, 1950).

10. Jarnés believed that when he writes a novel "the genius always takes life as his point of departure just as the ingenious [novelist] usually takes literature as his" (*Stefan Zweig*, p. 101). The truly gifted novelist starts with life, but does not end there. The "clever" novelist, always the target of Jarnés' scorn, starts with literature, i.e., with a picture of life which is not "true" and which has already undergone distortion. The element of distortion present in the literature used by the ingenious novelist for his point of departure is magnified by the distortion inherent in his novelistic process. Hence, the product is at two removes from life and incapable of giving a "true" picture of the age to later generations.

11. See *Escuela de libertad.*, p. 28. Jarnés' commitment, broader than the advocacy of the claims of a given party or faction, is seen

clearly in this comment: "To be a pacifist is to be nothing. In a time of peace, it can be comic. In time of war, it's very difficult not to consider [the pacifist] a coward. . . . We must wish for a world in which men have the strength to defend reason" (*Stefan Zweig*, p. 70).

12. A recent study by an American Catholic explores the subject in some detail in certain modern writers. See John Devlin, *Spanish Anti-Clericalism* (New York: Las Américas Publishing Co., 1966).

13. "Estampas antiguas," *RO*, XII, 36 (1926), 382. This was a review of Claudio Sánchez Albornoz, *Estampas de la vida en León hace mil años.*

14. "[Review of] Leon Frobenius, *El decamerón negro*," *RO*, VIII, 24 (1925), 393-94.

15. Madrid: Espasa-Calpe, 1929. This was the second in a series entitled "Vidas españolas del siglo XIX." The biography is based on historical documents Jarnés consulted in various archives. The series also included biographies by Antonio Espina, Antonio Marichalar, José María Salaverría, Pío Baroja, and Martín Luis Guzmán.

16. "Estampas antiguas," p. 383.

17. "[Review of] James Joyce, *El artista adolescente, RO*, XIII, 39 (1926), 382.

18. *Sobre la gracia artística* (Madrid: Blas, 1932), p. 9.

19. *Cartas al Ebro*, p. 38.

20. Jarnés wrote in 1942 that Disney was the favorite of the muses and "our own favorite in this generation" (*Stefan Zweig*, p. 118).

21. See Guillermo de Torre, *Historia de las literaturas de vanguardia*, p. 256.

22. The situation prevailed in America as well as in Europe. In a 1925 "advertisement" for H. L. Mencken, Kenneth Burke proclaimed: "We want smirks instead of piety." Matthew Josephson, *Life Among the Surrealists* (New York: Holt, Rinehart and Winston, 1962), ill. facing p. 149.

23. Review of Giraudoux, p. 115. See Note 5 above.

24. "Acuarelas de una exposición," *RO*, XVII, 49 (1927), 124.

25. The people walking in Madrid's Puerta del Sol "keep uncovering undulating, broken trajectories, mixtures of angles and curves" (*Don Alvaro o la fuerza del tino*, p. 32).

26. Although we have not done any statistical analysis of the prose, we offer the following as typical of the results such an analysis might produce. In *El professor inútil* (new ed.) the terms for "vibration" and related ideas occur with particular contextual meaning on these pages: 105, 106, 110, 131, 148, 149, 154, 159, 197, 230, and 255. Terms relating to "shyness" similarly occur on pages: 87, 97-98, 102, 109, 117, 118, 119, 147, 236, 252, and 255. Almost any of Jarnés' novels, because of their highly stylized prose, could provide useful data for statistical

analysis. Such analysis optimally would reveal and enlarge upon the thematic material we present in this chapter.

27. Cf. this description of Julio walking: he makes his feet "describe beautiful parabolas on the flashing stones" (*The Paper Guest*, p. 12).

28. In this novel, instructions for the application of makeup according to the particular shape of the woman's face are called "advanced studies of facial geometry" (*Theory of the Top-String*, p. 122). Or, the same image in another context: after the hero has slept with Paula, she puts on her makeup: "She wants to correct her three dimensions. To rectify by means of pure geometry what frantic love has disarranged" (*Paula and Paulette*, p. 149).

29. In "Años de aprendizaje y alegría," he had written of the "plastic energy, the epidermal seduction" of Goya, and the "dense musculature" of the prose of Gracián (pp. 12-13). Elsewhere, he called Goya "our diabolical Aragonese" and "that jokester from Fuendetodos" (*Vivien and Merlin*, 2nd ed., p. 10).

30. "Preámbulo. Un lírico de acción," in Jarnes' edition of Unamuno, *Páginas líricas* (México: Ediciones Mensaje, 1943), p. 19.

31. Angel Flores, "Introduction," to the selection by Jarnés in *Great Spanish Short Stories* (New York: Dell Publishing Co., 1962), p. 223.

32. "Los pies, el pie," *RO*, XVII, 50 (1927), 244.

33. See Guillermo de Torre, *Literaturas europeas de vanguardia*, pp. 58-59; and the same author's *Historia de las literaturas de vanguardia*, pp. 247-55.

34. In his review of Joyce's *El artista adolescente*, Jarnés wished to follow "that twisting line which the Irish schoolboy kept tracing on the sensitive plates of Art." See p. 384 of the review, *RO*, XIII, 39 (1926).

Chapter Five

1. *Corriente alterna* (México: Siglo XXI Editores, 1967), p. 8.

2. The sole exception might be Julio in his role as conspirator in *The Red and the Blue*. But as we have pointed out, Julio is no fervent Marxist, and cannot kill the lieutenant when he ought.

3. Cf. this remark by Wayne Booth: "The convenient but ultimately ridiculous notions that all concessions to the public are equally base, that the public itself is base, and that the author himself is not a member of 'the public,' can be as harmful as the desire to become a best seller at all costs." *The Rhetoric of Fiction*, p. 396.

4. His rejections were individualized and not made in the name of anyone else or of any group. Hence, when it suited him personally to accept the thing once rejected, he could do so without recanting

greatly from principle or in public (e.g., when he resumed active service in the army during the Second Republic).

5. This group, which met regularly at the Algonquin Hotel in New York in the late 1920's and 1930's, was comprised of the following writers: Franklin P. Adams, Robert Benchley, Heywood Broun, Marc Connelly, George S. Kaufman, Dorothy Parker, Harold Ross, and Alexander Woollcott.

6. Cf. Ortega's statement that the new art was "an art of privilege, of nobility of nerves, of instinctive aristocracy. Wherever the young muses appear, the masses trample them" (*La deshumanización del arte*, p. 355).

7. *Man's Hope*, tr. Stuart Gilbert and Alastair Macdonald (New York: Bantam Books, 1968), p. 212.

Selected Bibliography

Throughout the bibliography, the *Revista de Occidente* is abbreviated as *RO*.

PRIMARY SOURCES

A. Novels, Short Stories, Essays, and Biographies Published in Book Form by Jarnés, and Plays of His Which Were Produced.

1924   *Mosén Pedro (Father Pedro)*, Córdoba: Biblioteca Patria. A biographical portrait of Jarnés' brother, a rural priest.

1925   *"El hérve de la Legión," Los contemporáneos*, 7 May 1925. A three-act comedy, written with López Rienda; produced in 1925 in Madrid, by the Francisco Fuentes Company.

1926   *El profesor inútil (The Useless Professor)*, Madrid: Espasa-Calpe; new (2nd) ed.: *ibid.*, 1934, Jarnés' first novel and the one which gained him immediate fame.

1927   *Ejercicios (Exercises)*, Madrid: Cuadernos Literarios. A collection of short essays on fictional method.

1928   *El convidado de papel (The Paper Guest)*, Madrid: Historia Nueva. 2nd ed.: Madrid: Espasa-Calpe, 1935. A novel about seminary life in Zaragoza in the early twentieth century.

1929   *Locura y muerte de nadie (The Madness and Death of Nobody)*, Madrid: Ediciones Oriente. 2nd ed.: in *Las mejores novelas contemporáneas*, ed. Joaquín de Entrambasaguas, (Barcelona: Planeta, 1961), vol. VII, 1379-1564. A novel about the anguish of a man who has no personality.

      Paula y Paulita (Paula and Paulette), Madrid: Revista de Occidente. A novel about amorous encounters at a resort.

      Salón de estío (Summer Salon), Madrid: La Gaceta Literaria. A group of four stories ridiculing the excesses of Romantic passion.

      Sor Patrocinio: la monja de las llagas (Sister Patrocinius: The Nun of the Stigmata), Madrid: Espasa-Calpe. 2nd ed.: *ibid.*, 1930; 3rd ed.: *ibid.*, 1936. A biography of a nineteenth-century Spanish nun.

1930   *Teoría del zumbel (Theory of the Top-String)*, Madrid: Espasa-

Calpe. A novel about the experiences of a young roué.

Viviana y Merlín: leyenda (The Legend of Vivien and Merlin), Madrid: Ediciones Ulises. 2nd ed., ill.: Madrid: Espasa-Calpe, 1936. A re-creation of the Arthurian tale.

1931 *Escenas junto a la muerte (Scenes on the Brink of Death)*, Madrid: Espasa-Calpe. A novel recounting experiences of a would-be suicide.

Rúbricas: nuevos ejercicios (Flourishes: New Exercises), Madrid: Biblioteca Atlántico. Short essays on art; a continuation of *Ejercicios* (1927).

Zumalacárregui: el caudillo romántico (Zumalacárregui: The Romantic Chieftain), Madrid: Espasa-Calpe. A biography of the nineteenth-century Spanish political figure.

1932 *Lo rojo y lo azul: homenaje a Stendhal (The Red and the Blue: Homage to Stendhal)*, Madrid: Espasa-Calpe. A novel about life in the Spanish army in the 1920's and 1930's.

Sobre la gracia artística (On Artistic Grace), Madrid: Blas. A lecture on the role of grace and humor in art.

"Folletín." A comedy produced in Madrid on 3 June, at the Muñoz Seca Theater.

1933 *Fauna contemporánea: ensayos breves (Contemporary Animal Life: Short Essays)*, Madrid: Espasa-Calpe. A group of thirty-three satirical sketches of eleven common types of men, e.g., the parasite, the cynic, the coward, the agitator.

1934 *Cardenio: monodrama (Cardenius: Monodrama)*, Eco, Madrid: 2nd ed.: México: M. N. Lira, 1940. A monologue, produced in September, 1939, in Mexico City.

Vida de San Alejo (The Life of St. Alexis), Madrid· Ed. Literaria. A retelling of the life of the saint.

1935 *Castelar: hombre del Sinaí (Castelar: the Man from the Sinai)*, Madrid: Espasa-Calpe. A biography of the nineteenth-century Spanish political figure.

Feria del libro (Book Fair), Madrid: Espasa-Calpe. A series of appreciations and critiques of such writers as Unamuno, Gabriel Miró, Molière, Rousseau, Giraudoux, D. H. Lawrence, Aldous Huxley, Spranger, and Dostoevsky.

Libro de Esther (The Book of Esther), Madrid: Espasa-Calpe. 2nd ed.: Barcelona: José Janés, 1948. A series of conversations on art; comments on Goethe, Nietzsche, Max Aub, Stendhal, Benjamin Constant, Pirandello.

Tántalo: farsa (Tantalus: A Farce), Madrid: Signo. A farce about a playwright whose doctor forbids him to attend the theater.

1936 *Cita de ensueños: figuras del cinema (A Date with Illusion:*

Movie Personalities), Madrid: Galo Sáez. A series of essays on cinema, its techniques, and influence on literature; comments on such figures as Chaplin, Walt Disney, Greta Garbo, and Marlene Dietrich.

Doble agonía de Bécquer (The Double Agony of Becquer), Madrid: Espasa-Calpe. A biographical-critical essay on the lyric poetry of the nineteenth-century Spaniard.

Don Alvaro o la fuerza del tino (Don Alvaro or the Power of Good Aim), Madrid: Editores Reunidos. A novelette about a stain on a family's honor.

1940   *Cartas al Ebro: biografía y crítica (Letters to the Ebro: Biography and Criticism)*, México: La Casa de España en México. A series of short essays, some dating from the 1920's, on the dehumanization of art, and on the contributions of Jarnés' generation to art and literature.

La novia del viento (The Wind's Sweetheart), México: Ed. Cultura. A novel based in part on *Salón de estío* (1929).

1942   *Don Vasco de Quiroga, obispo de Utopía (Vasco de Quiroga: Bishop of Utopia)*, México: Ed. Atlántida. A biography of the sixteenth-century Spanish bishop of Michoacán.

Escuela de libertad: siete maestros (School for Freedom: Seven Teachers), México: Ed. Continental. Short biographies of Bolívar, Hidalgo, Lincoln, Martí, San Martín, Sucre, and Washington.

Manuel Acuña: poeta de su siglo (Manuel Acuña: Poet of His Age), México: Ed. Xóchitl. A biographical and critical sketch of the nineteenth-century Mexican poet.

Orlando el pacífico (Orlando the Calm), México: [PEN Collection]. A short (47 pp.) fairy tale.

Stefan Zweig: cumbre apagada, retrato (Stefan Zweig: Portrait of a Departed Master), México: Editorial Proa. A biographical-critical sketch of the twentieth-century Austrian writer.

1943   *Venus dinámica (Dynamic Venus)*, México: Editorial Proa. A novel based in part on *Don Alvaro o la fuerza del tino* (1936).

1944   *Cervantes: bosquejo biográfico (Cervantes: Biographical Sketch)*, México: Ediciones Nuevas. A short biography of the author of *Don Quixote*.

Constelación de Friné (Friné's Constellation), México: Editorial Proa. A "Grecian rhapsody" published under the pseudonym of Julio Aznar.

1946   *Ariel disperso (Ariel in Flight)*, México: Stylo. A series of essays, with a prologue by José Vasconcelos, on Spanish-American writers such as Borges, Carrera Andrade, Edwards Bello, Genaro Estrada, Mañach, Carlos Pellicer, Alfonso Reyes, Torres Bodet. The essays are reprinted here, having been published in the 1920's and 1930's.

1948 *Eufrosina o la gracia (Euphrosyne or Grace)*, Barcelona: José Janés. A series of dialogues on the role of grace and humor in art, written in 1938, and expanded from his *Sobre la gracia artística* (1932).

B. Short Stories, Articles, Book Reviews, Prologues, Translations, and Editions by Jarnés.

Jarnés' articles and book reviews number over 350. Extensive, though not complete, lists of them may be consulted in Fuentes, "La obra de Benjamín Jarnés," E. Segura Covarsi, and Merlin H. Foster (see Secondary Sources). Those listed here are those cited in the text and notes, together with several others of more than passing interest.

1. Short stories, articles, book reviews, prologues

"Acuarelas de una exposición," *RO*, XVII, 49 (1927), 123-25.
"Advertencia," in Julián Zugasti, *El banderolismo andaluz* (Madrid; Espasa-Calpe, 1934), pp. 7-8.
"Andrenio," in *Almanaque Literario, 1935,* ed. Guillermo de Torre, Miguel Pérez Ferrero, and E. Salazar Chapela (Madrid: Plutarco, 1935), pp. 222-226.
"Años de aprendizaje y alegría: (Nota autobiográfica)," in *Viviana y Merlín,* 1st ed., pp. 11-33.
"Antonio Machado," *España* [México], I, 15 (13 May 1944), 3.
"Bílbilis," *El Hijo Pródigo,* [México], V, 16 (15 July 1944), 26-31.
"El cántaro," *Sur,* III, 7 (1933), 110-29.
"Carta a la autora," in Paulita Brook, *Entre cuatro paredes (teatro)* (México: [Talleres Gráficos de la Nación], 1942), pp. 9-11.
"David y sus amigos: (Prólogo)," in Mariano Viñuales, *Blanquito* (México: Humanidad, 1943), pp. [7-14].
"La diligencia," in Antonio Espina *et al.,* eds., *Las siete virtudes* ([Santiago de Chile], Zig-Zag, n.d.), pp. 127-49.
"Discurso a Herminia," *RO*, XLI, 122 (1933), 166-96.
"Estambul, la sinuosa," *RO*, XIX, 56 (1928), 292-300.
"Estampas antiguas," *RO*, XII, 36 (1926), 380-85.
"De estrategia literaria," *RO*, XXX, 90 (1930), 370-74.
"Una falsa falsilla," *RO*, XXI, 62 (1928), 243-45.
"Fe de erratas," in *Cartas al Ebro,* pp. 25-31.
"Fernando el político," *Filosofía y Letras* [México], III, 5 (January-March, 1942), 83-92.

"La flor azul," *Cuadernos Americanos*, 1, 3, 3, (May-June, 1942), 211-18.

"Francisco de Goya," *España* [México], 1, 11 (15 April, 1944), 3.

"Heráclito y la ondina," *Cuadernos Americanos*, II, 9, 3 (May-June, 1943), 224-35.

"Libros sin género," *RO*, XXXII, 95 (1931), 205-9.

"Locura y muerte de nadie," *RO*, XIX, 55 (1928), 1-39.

"La mesa de los poetas feos: Novela escénica," *Et Caetera* [Guadalajara], I, 1 (January-March, 1950), 25-41.

"La musa de ébano," *RO*, XVIII, 52 (1927), 109-12.

"Nota crítica," in Manuel Andújar, *Cristal herido* (México: Editorial Isla, 1945), pp. [525-26].

"Nota preliminar," in *Paula y Paulita*, pp. 13-19.

"Una novela," in *Cartas al Ebro*, pp. 87-91.

"El novelista en la novela," *RO*, XLII, 125 (1933), 230-33.

"El novelista pujante," in *In memoriam: Libro-homenaje al inmortal novelista V. Blasco Ibáñez* (Valencia: Prometeo, 1929), pp. 201-205.

"Paula y Paulita," *RO*, X, 29 (1925), 129-60.

"Los pies, el pie," *RO*, XVII, 50 (1927), 239-44.

"Posdata," in Manuel Delgado, *Reloj de arena*, Prefacio del Lic. Manuel Múzquiz (México: Biblioteca Hoy, 1941), pp. 145-46.

"Preámbulo. Un lírico de acción," in Miguel de Unamuno, *Páginas líricas*, ed. Benjamín Jarnés (México: Ediciones Mensaje, 1943), pp. 9-21.

"Prólogo," in Margarita Ferreras, *Pez en la tierra* (Madrid: Impresores Concha Méndez y Manuel Altolaguirre, 1932), pp. 9-13.

"Ramón del Valle-Inclán," *España* [México], I, 19 (10 June 1944), 5.

"Red invisible," *Sur*, VIII, 40 (1938), 17-29.

"Revistas nuevas," *RO*, XV, 44 (1927), 263-66.

"[Review of] J. L. Borges, *Inquisiciones*," *RO*, IX, 25 (1925), 125-27.

"[Review of] Jean Cocteau, *Poésie*," *RO*, IX, 27 (1925), 391-95.

"[Review of] León Frobenius, *El decamerón negro*," *RO*, VIII, 24 (1925), 393-97.

"[Review of] Jean Giraudoux, *Bella*," *RO*, XII, 34 (1926), 112-16.

"[Review of] Ramón Gómez de la Serna, *La quinta de Palmira*," *RO*, X, 28 (1925), 112-17.

"[Review of] Gerardo Hauptman, *La prodigiosa isla de las damas*," *RO*, X, 29 (1925), 247-50.

"[Review of] James Joyce, *El artista adolescente*," *RO*, XIII, 39 (1926), 382-86.

"El río fiel," *RO*, VIII, 23 (1925), 145-69.

"Ruinas en España," *Hora de España* [Valencia], XVI (1938), 71-78.

"Sherwood Anderson," *RO*, XX, 60 (1928), 349-57.

"Teoría del zumbel," *RO*, XXVII, 79 (1930), 11-39.

"Unamuno, intérprete y nervio de España," in José Moreno Villa *et al.*, *Retablo hispánico* (México: Editorial Clavileño, 1946), pp. 17-24.

2. Translations

Bey, Mohammed Essad, *La policía secreta de los Soviets. Historia de G. P. U. (1917-1933)* (Madrid: Espasa-Calpe, 1935).

El cantar de Roldán (Madrid: Revista de Occidente, 1926; 2nd ed.: *ibid.*, 1945; 3rd ed.: *ibid.*, 1948; 4th ed.: *ibid.*, 1963).

Germain, Auguste, *Los paraísos* (México: Editorial Leyenda [1945]).

Gourmont, Rémy, de, *Historias mágicas* (México: Editorial Leyenda, 1944).

Jonson, Ben, *Volpone, La Farsa* [Madrid], III, 120 [December 28, 1929], 5-62.

Ognew, Nicolás [pseud. of Mikhail Grigorévich Rozanov], *El diario de Costia Riabtzev* (Madrid: Espasa-Calpe, 1929), trans. from Swedish in collaboration with Tatiana Enco de Valero.

Périot, Maurice, *Temperamento y personalidad* (México: Editorial Esculapio, 1944).

Philippe, Charles Louis, *Bubu de Montparnasse* (Madrid: Biblioteca Nueva, 1932).

Polo, Marco, *El millón* ([México]: Galatea [n.d., but probably 1945]).

Prévost, L'Abbé, *Historia de Manon Lescaut y del Caballero del Grieux* ([México]: Editorial Leyenda, [1945]).

Remarque, Erich Maria, *Sin novedad en la frente* (Madrid: Espasa-Calpe, 1929), in collaboration with Eduardo Foertsch.

Strowska, Susana, *Leyendas polacas* (Madrid: Revista de Occidente, 1928, 2nd ed.: *ibid.*, 1944).

Tuffrau, Paul, *La leyenda de Guillermo de Orange* (Madrid: Espasa-Calpe, 1925).

3. Editions

Enciclopedia de la literatura (México: Editora Central [1947]), 6 vols.

El libro de oro de los niños, literary ed., Benjamín Jarnés, artistic ed., Luis Doporto; prologues by Juana de Ibarbourou and Gabriela Mistral (México: Editorial Acrópolis, 1946), 6 vols.

La sal del mundo: Recolección de notas de Benjamín Jarnés (México: E.D.I.A.P.S.A., 1940).

El sueño de las calaveras (México: E.D.I.A.P.S.A. [n.d.]).

La taberna por vecina (México: E.D.I.A.P.S.A., 1940).

Unamuno, Miguel de, *Páginas escogidas* (México: Secretaría de Educación Pública, 1947).

Unamuno, Miguel de, *Páginas líricas* (México: Ediciones Mensaje, 1943).

C.   Jarnés' fugitive bibliograph.

In addition to the works cited above, and to those in other bibliographies to which we have already referred the reader, we would like to list those fugitive works of Jarnés' of which we are aware. In each case, the title is given with an indication of whether the work was said to have been published or not. The dates listed are those of works by Jarnés whose frontispieces or jackets referred to the fugitive work. The names of other authors refer to works, listed in Secondary Sources of this bibliography, in which the fugitive work was mentioned.

While some of these titles denote books which Jarnés wrote but did not publish, many of them denote works which he either had begun and never finished, or which he merely planned to write. In any case, the list is offered in the hope that a beginning may be made on the project of disentangling the rather complicated Jarnés bibliography and establishing a trustworthy list of all the works in his canon.

1. "Amor bajo tres lunas"—"in preparation," 1929.
2. "Antinóo en la pista"—"in preparation," 1940.
3. "El aprendiz de brujo" [novel]—Entrambasaguas says Jarnés' widow has the unpublished ms.
4. "El bosque de Titania"—"in preparation," 1940.
5. "La casa de los pájaros" [a novel about the Spanish Civil War]—"unpublished," Fuentes, "La obra de Benjamín Jarnés."
6. "Circe en la esquina"—"in press," 1940.
7. "Clío al desnudo"—"in preparation," 1940.
8. "Correo de ultramar" [brief essays]—"in press," 1940.
9. "Desierto profanado" [novel]—Entrambasaguas says Jarnés' widow has the unpublished ms.
10. "Ejercicios" [new enlarged ed.]—"to appear soon," 1940.
11. "Elogio de la impureza"—"to appear soon," 1934 and 1935.
12. "En mitad de la calle"—"in press," 1940.
13. "Escombros" [travel sketches]—"unpublished," Fuentes, "La obra de Benjamín Jarnés."
14. "Examen de ingenuos [sic]" [brief essays]—Entrambasaguas says Jarnés' widow has the unpublished ms.; he has "ingenios."
15. "Fábrica de viento"—"in press," 1940; this was also the title given to the first part of *Tántalo, farsa* (1935).
16. "La feria de los libros" [2nd ed.]—"in preparation," 1940.
17. "Figuras y paisajes" [criticism]—Entrambasaguas says Jarnés' widow has the unpublished ms.
18. "Galatea desdeñosa"—"in preparation," 1940.
19. "Libro de Ruth"—"unpublished," 1944.

20. "Luz y taquígrafos"—"in preparation," 1940.
21. "Miguel Servet" [biography]—"to appear soon," 1934 and 1935.
22. "Mosén Pedro" [new enlarged ed.]—"to appear soon," 1940.
23. "La novia de Otelo" [monodrama]—"unpublished," 1940.
24. "Pauta y arabesco" [brief essays]—"in preparation," 1929, "unpublished," 1931 and 1940.
25. "El profesor inútil" [3rd ed.]—"to appear soon," 1940.
26. "Un pueblo y un hombre" [novel]—"to appear soon," 1930.
27. "Reparto de gloria"—"in preparation," 1940.
28. "Rúbricas" [new enlarged ed.]—"to appear soon," 1940.
29. "Rutas de luz"—"in press," Fresco.
30. "Sala de espera" [monodrama]—"published" 1942, listed by Entrambasaguas as published in 1936; we could find no copy.
31. "El sagaz Ulises"—"in preparation," 1940.
32. "Su línea de fuego" [novel]—"published" 1940 and 1942.
33. "Tanit, llama y rocío: (Vida íntima de San Agustín)"—"in preparation," 1944.
34. "Tiro al blanco"—"in preparation," 1940.
35. "Torre y alfil"—"to appear soon," 1929.
36. "Viaje a un dívan" [novel]—"published" 1940 and 1942.
37. "Vida amorosa de Quevedo"—"to appear soon," 1929.

Titles numbered 2, 4, 6, 7, 12, 15, 18, 20, 27, 31, and 34 were announced as parts of a series under the general title "Libros de Buen Humor" to be issued by E.D.I.A.P.S.A. in Mexico City. Each volume was to be a collection of humorous anecdotes edited by Jarnés, each on a different theme. Three other titles in the series, *The Spice of Life*, *The Playboys' Dream* and *The Neighborhood Tavern*, were actually published and are listed in part B of this bibliography.

SECONDARY SOURCES

The following list consists of selected bio-bibliographical and critical articles on Jarnés, works useful for an understanding of the author's times, as well as other works referred to in the text and notes. In view of the more than 150 articles and book reviews dealing with Jarnés and his work cited by Entrambasaguas which appeared in Spanish newspapers before 1950, any attempt at a complete bibliography of Jarnés criticism is beyond the scope of this book. The items of Jarnés criticism included here are, we believe, among the least ephemeral and most relevant in the literature.

AGUILERA CERNI, VICENTE. *Ortega y D'Ors en la cultura artística española* (Madrid: Editorial Ciencia Nueva, 1966).

ANDRÉS ÁLVAREZ, VALENTÍN. "Apunte autobiográfico," in *Naufragio en la sombra* (Madrid: Ediciones Ulises, 1930), pp. 7-22.

————. *Tararí* (Madrid: Espasa-Calpe, 1929).

[ARANA, JOSÉ RAMÓN, AND ANDÚJAR, MANUEL]. "Benjamín Jarnés," *Las Españas* [México], V, 13 (29 October 1949), 3.

ARJONA, DORIS KING. "*La voluntad* and *abulia* in Contemporary Spanish Ideology," *Revue Hispanique*, LXXIV (1928), 573-672.

ARROYO, CIRIACO MORÓN. "Algebra y logoritmo: Dos metáforas de Ortega y Gasset," *Hispania*, XLIX (1966), 232-37.

AUB, MAX. *Discurso de la novela española contemporánea* (México: El Colegio de México, 1945).

AYALA, FRANCISCO. "Proemio" [1949], to *La cabeza del cordero* (Buenos Aires: Compañía General Fabril Editora, 1962), pp. 27-36.

BAJARLÍA, JUAN JACOBO. *Literatura de vanguardia: Del 'Ulises' de Joyce y las escuelas poéticas* (Buenos Aires: Editorial Araujo, 1946).

BAQUERO GOYANES, MARIANO. *Problemas de la novela contemporánea* (Madrid: Ateneo, 2nd ed. 1956).

————. *Proceso de la novela actual* (Madrid: Ediciones Rialp, 1963).

BARINAGA FERNÁNDEZ, AGUSTO. *Movimientos literarios españoles en los siglos XIX y XX* (Madrid: Ed. Alhambra, 1964).

BAROJA [Y NESSI], PÍO. "Prólogo casi doctrinal sobre la novela" [1925], in *Obras completas* (Madrid: Biblioteca Nueva, 1948), IV, 307-27.

BLEIBERG, GERMÁN. "Benjamín Jarnés," in *Diccionario de literatura española*, eds. Germán Bleiberg and Julián Marías (Madrid: Revista de Occidente, 3rd rev. ed., 1964), pp. 424-25.

BODINI, VITTORIO. "Benjamín Jarnés," in *Grande Dizionario Enciclopedico* (Torino: Unione Tipografico, 2nd ed., 1957), VI, 1095.

BOOTH, WAYNE C. *The Rhetoric of Fiction* (Chicago and London: University of Chicago Press, 1961).

BRENAN, GERALD. *The Spanish Labyrinth* (Cambridge: Cambridge University Press, 1960).

BUERO VALLEJO, ANTONIO. "Obligada precisión acerca del imposibilismo," *Primer Acto*, July-August, 1960, 1-6.

BURKE, KENNETH. *Attitudes Toward History* (Boston: Beacon Press, 1961).

CAMUS, ALBERT. *Notebooks: 1935-1942*, tr. and ed. Philip Thody (New York: Knopf, 1963).

CHABÁS, JUAN. *Literatura española contemporánea: 1898-1950* (La Habana: Ed. Cultural, 1952).

CHACEL, ROSA. "Respuesta a Ortega: La novela no escrita," *Sur*, 241 (1956), 96-119.

CIENFUEGOS, SEBASTIÁN. "Le Roman en Espagne," tr. Pierre Gamarra, *Europe*, XXXVI (1958), 17-29.

CIRRE, JOSÉ FRANCISCO. *Forma y espíritu de una lírica española: Noticia sobre la renovación poética en España de 1920 a 1935* (México: Gráfica Panamericana, 1950).

COWLEY, MALCOLM. *Exile's Return* (New York: Viking Press, 1966).

CROSSMAN, RICHARD, ed. *The God That Failed* (London: Hamish Hamilton, 1950).

CRUZ OCAMPO, LUIS D. *L'Intellectualisation de l'art*, tr. Adolphe de Falgairolle (Paris: Editions "Le Livre Libre," 1931).

DEVLIN, JOHN. *Spanish Anti-Clericalism: A Study in Modern Alienation* (New York: Las Americas Publishing Co., 1966).

DOMENCHINA, JUAN JOSÉ. *Crónicas de Gerardo Rivera* (México: Ed. Centauro, 2nd ed., 1946).

ELLIS, KEITH. "El enfoque literario de la guerra civil española: Malraux y Ayala," in Francisco Ayala, *La cabeza del cordero* (Buenos Aires: Compañía General Fabril Editora, 1962), pp. 9-23.

ENTRAMBASAGUAS, JOAQUÍN DE. "Benjamín Jarnés," in *Las mejores novelas contemporáneas* (Barcelona: Planeta, 1961), VII, 1313-78.

ESPINA, ANTONIO. *Luna de copas* (Madrid: Espasa-Calpe, 1929).

_____. *El nuevo diantre* (Madrid: Espasa-Calpe, 1934).

_____. *Pájaro pinto* (Madrid: Espasa-Calpe, 1927).

_____. "[Review of] Benjamín Jarnés, *Libro de Esther*," *RO*, XLVIII, 142 (1935), 106-12.

FERNÁNDEZ-SANTOS, FRANCISCO. "Julián Marías y el 'liberalismo' o cómo se hace un diccionario de literatura," *Cuadernos de Ruedo Ibérico*, No. 1 *(June-July, 1965)*, 63-69.

FLORES, ANGEL, ed. *Great Spanish Short Stories* (New York: Dell Publishing Co., 1962).

FORSTER, E. M. *Aspects of the Novel* (New York: Harcourt, Brace, 1954).

FOSTER, MERLIN H. *An Index to Mexican Literary Periodicals* (New York and London: Scarecrow Press, 1966).

FRESCO, MAURICIO. *La emigración republicana española: Una victoria de México* (México: Editores Asociados, 1950).

FUENTES, VÍCTOR [FLOREAL]. "Benjamín Jarnés: Aproximaciones a su intimidad y creación," *Cuadernos Hispanoamericanos*, LXXII, 214 (1967), 33-40.

_____. "La obra de Benjamin Jarnés: Un estudio de su novelística y de su estética," unpublished Ph.D. theis, New York University, 1965.

GIL, ILDEFONSO MANUEL. "Ciudades y paisajes aragoneses en las novelas de Benjamin Jarnés," *Archivo de Filología Aragonesa* [Zaragoza] VI (1956), 87-114.

GIMÉNEZ CABALLERO, ERNESTO. *El Robinson literario de España: O la república de las letras* (Madrid: [Ediciones de Bibliófilo de] La Gaceta Literaria, 1932), vols. I-VI.

GÓMEZ DE LA SERNA, RAMÓN. "Sobre la novela," *Síntesis* [Buenos Aires], III (1929), 43-48.

GOYTISOLO, JUAN. *Problemas de la novela* (Barcelona: Seix-Barral, 1959).

GROSSVOGEL, DAVID I. *Limits of the Novel* (Ithaca: Cornell University Press, 1968).

GULLÓN, RICARDO. "Benjamín Jarnés," *Insula*, IV, 46 (15 October 1949), 8.

—————. "Inventario de medio siglo: II. Literatura española," *Insula*, V, 58 (15 October, 1950), 3, 6.

—————. "The Modern Spanish Novel," tr. Douglas M. Rogers, *Texas Quarterly*, IV (1961), 79-96.

—————. "Prosistas de la generación del '25," *Insula*, XII, 126 (15 May 1957), 1, 8.

IGLESIAS, CARMEN. "La controversia entre Baroja y Ortega acerca de la novela," *Hispanófila*, VII (1959), 41-50.

ILIE, PAUL. "Benjamín Jarnés: Aspects of the Dehumanized Novel," *PMLA*, LXXVI (1961), 247-53.

—————. "Futurism in Spain," *Criticism*, VI (1964), 201-11.

—————. *The Surrealist Mode in Spanish Literature* (Ann Arbor: The University of Michigan Press, 1968).

IRIZARRY, CARMEN. *The Thirty Thousand* (New York: Harcourt, Brace and World, 1966).

JOSEPHSON, MATTHEW. *Life Among the Surrealists* (New York: Holt, Rinehart and Winston, 1962).

KING, CHARLES L. "Sender's Spherical Philosophy," *PMLA*, LXIX (1954), 993-99.

LAFUENTE FERRARI, ENRIQUE. "Cuarenta años de deshumanización del arte," *RO*, 2nd series, I, 8 and 9 (1963), 313-26.

LAMANA, MANUEL. *La novela de la postguerra* (Bahía Blanca [Argentina]: Cuadernos del Sur, 1960).

LIVINGSTONE, LEON. "Ortega y Gasset's Philosophy of Art," *PMLA*, LXVII (1952), 609-54.

LUBBOCK, PERCY. *The Craft of Fiction* (New York: Viking Press, 1960).

LUZURIAGA, JORGE. "Sobre el exilio: 1939-1964," *RO*, 2nd series, II, 12 (1964), 345-48.

MALRAUX, ANDRÉ. *Man's Hope*, tr. Stuart Gilbert and Alastair Macdonald (New York: Bantam Books, 1968).
MARRA-LÓPEZ, JOSÉ. *Narrativa española fuera de España: 1939-1961* (Madrid: Guadarrama, 1963).
MARTÍNEZ, CARLOS. *Crónica de una emigración: La de los republicanos españoles en 1939* (México: Libro Mex, 1959).
McDONALD, E. CORDEL. "The Modern Novel as Viewed by Ortega," *Hispania*, XLII (1959), 475-81.
McLUHAN, MARSHALL. "Third Program in the Human Age," *Explorations*, 8 (1957), 16-19.
MONTESINOS, JOSÉ [FERNÁNDEZ]. "Modernismo, esperpentismo, o las dos evasiones," *RO*, 2nd series, IV, 44-45 (1966), 146-65.
MORENO VILLA, JOSÉ. *Vida en claro: Autobiografía* (México: El Colegio de México, 1944).
NORA, EUGENIO G. DE. *La novela española contemporánea: 1898-1960* (Madrid: Gredos, 3 vols., 1958-1962).
ONTAÑÓN, EDUARDO DE. *Viaje y aventura de los escritores de España* (México: Ediciones Minerva [1942]).
ORTEGA Y GASSET, JOSÉ. *La deshumanización del arte*, in *Obras completas* (Madrid: Revista de Occidente, 1947), III, 353-84.
_____. "Ensayo de estética a manera de prólogo," in *Obras completas* (Madrid: Revista de Occidente, 5th ed., 1961), VI, 247-64.
_____. *Ideas sobre la novela*, in *Obras completas* (Madrid: Revista de Occidente, 1947), III, 387-419.
_____. "Le temps, la distance et la forme chez Proust," *La Nouvelle Revue Française*, X, 112 (1923), 267-79.
PALENCIA, ISABEL DE. *Smouldering Freedom: The Story of the Spanish Republicans in Exile* (New York and Toronto: Longmans, Green and Co., 1945).
PAZ, OCTAVIO. *Corriente alterna* (México: Siglo XXI Editores, 1967).
PÉREZ, DARÍO. "Benjamín Jarnés," in *Figuras de España* (Madrid: Compañía Ibero-Americana de Publicaciones, 1930), pp. 269-83.
PUTNAM, SAMUEL. "Benjamín Jarnés y la deshumanización del arte," *Revista Hispánica Moderna*, II (1935-36), 17-21.
READ, HERBERT. "Mediodía y noche oscura: (Algunas observaciones sobre la filosofía del arte de Ortega y Gasset)," *RO*, 2nd series, IV, 40 (1966), 1-18.
ROBBE-GRILLET, ALAIN. *For a New Novel: Essays on Fiction*, tr. Richard Howard (New York: Grove Press, 1965).
RODRÍGUEZ-ALCALÁ, HUGO. "Un aspecto del antagonismo de Unamuno y Ortega," *Revista de la Universidad de Buenos Aires*, II (1957), 266-80.
ROGGIANO, ALFREDO A. "Estética y crítica literaria en Ortega y Gasset," *La Torre*, IV (1956), 337-59.

172   BENJAMÍN JARNÉS

SALAVERRÍA, JOSÉ. La intimidad literaria (Madrid: Ed. Calleja, 1919).
SALAZAR Y CHAPELA, ESTEBAN. "Literatura plana y literatura del
    espacio," RO, XV, 44 (1927), 280-88.
SALINAS, PEDRO. Vísperas del gozo (Madrid: Espasa-Calpe, 1926).
SCHWARTZ, KESSEL. "A Falaganist View of Golden Age Literature,"
    Hispania, XLIX (1966), 206-10.
SEGURA COVARSI, E[NRIQUE]. Indice de la Revista de Occidente
    (Madrid: Consejo Superior de Investigaciones Científicas, 1952).
SERRANO PONCELA, S[EGUNDO]. "La novela española contemporánea,"
    La Torre, I (1953), 105-28.
_____. "Razón y débito a Ortega y Gasset," in El secreto de Melibea
    y otros ensayos (Madrid: Taurus, 1956), pp. 213-30.
SHAW, D. L. "A Reply to 'Deshumanización'—Baroja on the Art of
    the Novel," Hispanic Review, XXV (1957), 105-11.
SILVA CASTRO, RAÚL. "Benjamín Jarnés," Atenea, XII, 58 (1929),
    247-62.
SMITH, LOIS ELWYN. "Mexico and the Spanish Republicans," Univer-
    sity of California Publications in Political Science, IV, 2 (1955),
    165-316.
TORRE, GUILLERMO DE. El fiel de la balanza (Madrid: Taurus, 1961).
_____. Historia de las literaturas de vanguardia (Madrid: Guadar-
    rama, 1965).
_____. "Las ideas estéticas de Ortega," Sur, 241 (1956), 79-89.
_____. Literaturas europeas de vanguardia (Madrid: Caro Raggio,
    1925).
_____. Problemática de la literatura (Buenos Aires: Losada, 2nd
    ed., 1958).
_____. Tríptico del sacrificio: Unamuno, García Lorca, Machado
    (Buenos Aires: Losada, 2nd ed., 1960).
_____. Miguel Pérez Ferrero, and E. Salazar Chapela, Eds.,
    Alamanaque Literario, 1935 (Madrid: Plutarco, 1935).
TORRES BODET, JAIME. Tiempo de arena, in Obras escogidas (México:
    Fondo de Cultura Económica, 1961), pp. 191-384.
VIDELA, GLORIA. El ultraísmo: Estudios sobre movimientos poéticos
    de vanguardia en España (Madrid: Gredos, 1963).
WEBER, FRANCES. "An Approach to Ortega's Idea of Culture: The
    Concept of Literary Genre," Hispanic Review, XXXII (1964),
    142-56.
WINECOFF, JANET. "The Spanish Novel from Ortega to Castellet:
    Dehumanization of the Artist," Hispania, L (1967), 35-43.
ZUBIZARRETA, ARMANDO E. Unamuno en su nivola (Madrid: Taurus,
    1960).
ZULETA [ALVAREZ], EMILIA [PUCEIRO] DE. "Benjamín Jarnés," Uni-
    versidad [Santa Fe, Argentina], LV (1963), 21-60.

————. *Historia de la crítica española contemporánea* (Madrid: Gredos 1966).

————. "La novela de Benjamín Jarnés," *Insula*, XVIII, 203 (1963), 7.

————. "Revisión de Benjamín Jarnés en su obra crítica," *Papeles de Son Armadans*, XLII, 126 (1966), 125-36.

Index